Dedicated to the creative trailblazers throughout history who have touched our souls and inspired us to help bring forth the world we want to live in.

"What a long strange trip it's been."
– Jerry Garcia

My OUT OF THE BLUE Stories

One Man's Journey Through Life

Written and published by Scott Seldin

My Out of the Blue Stories

Edited by Gordana Vantacic

Interior formatted by
E.M. Tippetts Book Designs, Santa Fe NM

Other Books by Scott Seldin

Yes, Boss, 1982, Blythe-Pennington LTD

Mentoring Human Potential, 2011, IUniverse

Contents

Introduction

I've always loved stories. When I was a boy, sharing a room with my younger brother Clem, before we fell asleep each night, I made up a story as I told it to him.

My love of stories continued into adulthood and led to a Master of Fine Arts in Creative Writing, two published books and now, *My Out of the Blue Stories*.

Before reading this book, you might want to know why I wrote it. Here are four reasons.

First, I would like my friends and family to read my stories because I think doing so will bring me closer to them. When I was a teenager, my grandfather, Israel Seldin, sent a lengthy handwritten letter to my brothers and me, titled, "My life in your hands."

The letter, written a few years before he died, described his family's life as Jews in 19th century Russia. Reading his letter gave me a deeper understanding of who he was. It also helped me gain insight into my father growing up as his father's son.

Israel Seldin wrote: "My mother died at the age of 32. A cold, pneumonia, and dead. No doctor. Four young children left. A girl of eleven, a boy of eight, myself, five, and a baby one year old. Thirty days after my mother's death, my father remarried. He could not help it. I missed the most valuable gift a child can have – mother love. The lack of mother love left a vacant spot in my makeup.

The town where I was born was very small, about fifty houses, with about sixty families, all Jewish, surrounded by not friendly Christian villages. What our town lacked in numbers it made up for with poverty. If a family had a shack to live in, a small garden to raise vegetables, a cow and some chickens, that family was considered well to do. Our family had all that and my father's profession, instructor in Talmud, paid him about two hundred rubles a year."

In 1966, during my freshman year at college, the seed for my second reason to write my stories was planted in the poetry section of a bookstore in Washington, D.C. I randomly pulled a book from a shelf — T*he Love Poems* of *Elizabeth Sargent* — opened it to the first page and read the signed inscription: "To an unknown friend."

I bought the book without reading another word, and when I read Elizabeth Sargent's poems, her voice spoke to me as an unknown friend.

If we are strangers, you are my unknown friend, and *My Out of the Blue Stories* is written with you in mind.

My third reason: I wrote this book for myself. These chronologically presented stories gave me an opportunity to understand them as an inter-related continuum of stories.

And fourth: I've had a colorful life, with many life-shaping experiences that I believe are worth sharing. I suspect that you, too, have had a colorful life, with stories that others would like to read. I hope that this book will inspire you to write them.

The names of people mentioned in my stories have been changed, or are part of a public record, or names are used, knowing that the people mentioned would approve.

None of my stories have been embellished. Each was written with veracity and vivid memories as my only guides.

Henry James once wrote, "What is character but the determination of incident? What is incident but the illustration of character?"

Here are my stories for you.

February 6, 1945

I'm living in a sack of amniotic love

Though I don't remember being in utero, I imagine it is dark and I'm living in a sack of amniotic love. My timeless world is sweet and secure. I explore it gently with my legs and hands, comforted by muffled sounds.

Suddenly, the world I've been living in for seven and a half months disappears when my mother is told that her father has died. I'm immersed in her grief and time begins for me.

March 15, 1945

I blink into existence

I'm born and named Charles Scott Seldin, though I'll be called Scotty until high school, when everyone starts calling me Scott.

On my first day of life, my mother tells me many years later, she tried to breast feed me and stopped after I got sick from the grief in her milk, caused by her father's death.

I'm loved and wonderfully cared for by my older brother, Peter, and my mother and father — my family. We live in an apartment in Brooklyn, New York.

Summer, 1947

A monkey dances on the sidewalk below

I'm two years old. Late afternoon, I hear the sound of music below our apartment's open window that overlooks a sidewalk and trees that line the street. I stand on tip toes and below me I see a man playing an organ grinder while a monkey dances next to him, holding a cup. I'm entranced.

1948

A bubble and a cup of brook

My father is in our Brooklyn apartment bathroom. He has lathered his face to shave. I walk into the bathroom and say hi. He smiles and blows a soap bubble that floats in the air and bursts. The surprise delights me and I think, if my father can do that, he can do anything.

My brother Clem is born. I'm three years old with an older and younger brother. Life is very good.

Summers, my family travels to a cabin near Peekskill, New York, about forty-five miles north of New York City. My mother's parents bought the cabin before the stock market crash of 1929. A dirt road leads to the cabin, cutting through tall grass and wildflowers.

One morning, my mother holds my hand and leads me down wood steps to a brook. She dips a large metal cup into the water and shows me several minnows swimming in the cup's brook water. I love seeing country life swimming as minnows in a cup of brook with the same aliveness that I see everywhere I look – in the trees, the rabbits, bugs, birds, butterflies. I'm delighted by everything that walks, crawls, flies, or grows in the ground. I feel connected.

Spring, 1949

Is there a law?

My mother tells me, years later, that when I was four, while sitting at our dinner table in Brooklyn, Peter told me to eat the spinach on my plate. I asked him, "Is there a law?"

Fall, 1949

Do that again

Clem and I sit on a stoop outside the building where we live in Brooklyn. An elderly man walks slowly toward us and stops, facing us. "Hello boys," he says.

I say, "Hello."

He asks, "Do you want to see something amazing?"

I say, "Yes."

The man reaches into his mouth, takes out his false teeth and shows them to us. He puts his teeth back in his mouth and I say, "Do that again."

He smiles and says, "Sorry, boys. I only do that once a day." He walks away. I try to take my teeth out of my mouth.

Summer, 1950

The sound of Nanny's voice

Our family moves from Brooklyn and rents a house near the Croton Dam in Croton-on-Hudson, New York, thirty-five miles north of New York City. We can walk from the house down a flight of wood steps to a dock and a large lake.

My grandmother, "Nanny," as she is called, is visiting, staying with us in the house for a few days. We all love Nanny. She is gentle, loving and kind.

During her visit, my brother Peter and I are play-wrestling on the dock. Nanny walks down the stairs and calls to us with distress in her voice. "Don't fight, boys. Please don't fight." Her voice is so gentle and loving and upset that I stop wrestling. Peter stops also. We feel what we hear in her voice. It hurts her to see us fighting, even if we're play-fighting. I'm changed by the sound of her voice.

Early September, 1950, kindergarten

You're a very good boy, Scotty

I begin Kindergarten in Croton and during our first day, my class is given a tour of the school building we're in, built in 1940 with money from the Work Projects Administration.

We're shown the gymnasium, the library, the lunch room and the lost and found, which is in the principal's office, directly across from the door that leads outside to the playground.

A friendly woman in this office tells us about the lost and found. She says if we find anything special that doesn't belong to us, we should bring it to her. And if we lose something special, we should stop by to see if someone found it and brought it there.

That afternoon, my class is given free time on the playground. I walk around and notice a stone that's covered with flecks of silver-colored mica. I pick up the stone and, to my eyes, it looks as if it has tiny stars embedded in it. I take the stone to the lost and found and give it to the woman who talked to us earlier that day.

I tell her, "I found this on the playground. I think someone lost it."

She smiles and takes the stone. "Thank you very much. What is your name?"

"Scotty Seldin."

She tells me, "You're a very good boy, Scotty, for bringing this to the lost and found." She takes my hand and says, "Now let's go back to the playground."

The following day, I find another stone with lots of mica in it. I bring the stone to the lost and found and the same woman says, "Hello, Scotty. I see you've brought another beautiful stone with mica in it. Thank you. I like it very much, but no one lost it. Stones with mica in them are usually left outside. The lost and found is for anything we find that belongs to someone else — things like hats and coats and gloves and books. You can put the two stones you found back where you found them, or you can take them home and show them to your family and keep them. Would you like to do that?"

"Yes."

I take the stones home and show them to my family. Everyone thinks they're beautiful and my mother puts them on a night table next to my bed in the room I share with Clem.

1951

Our own home

My parents buy a one hundred and fifty-year-old former Quaker meeting house in Croton-on-Hudson. Seventy-five years after it was built, the meeting house became a one-room school house.

1952, second grade

I commit a federal crime

I've learned that mail sent to people is delivered and left in their mailboxes until they take it out.

After school one day, I walk with Clem along the country road that passes in front of our house. We stop several houses away. I open our neighbor's mailbox, remove the mail and randomly take a letter, returning the rest to the mailbox.

A woman leans out the second-story window of the house and calls to us, "Hey! What are you kids doing?" I call back to her, "I'm the new mailman."

She pauses, then shuts the window. Clem and I walk back to our house. Alone in the bedroom I share with him, I open the envelope and take out a folded letter with a five-dollar bill inside.

The next Saturday, I take the five dollars with me in a pocket when my mother drives me to my friend Ritchie Robbins' house for some play time. In his room, I show him the money, which is more than either of us has ever held in our hands. Ritchie's mother walks into his bedroom as we're looking at it. She asks me where I got the five dollars. I tell her it was in an envelope that I took from a neighbor's mailbox.

When my mother comes to pick me up at Ritchie's house, his mother tells her about the five dollars. On the drive home, my mother asks me how I got the money. I tell her. She asks if I know that it's against the law to take someone else's mail. I say I know. She asks, "Do you promise to never do that again?" I promise and say I'm sorry.

My mother returns the envelope, the letter and the five dollars to our neighbor, with an apology from both of us.

1952

A bird on my head

The school bus drops me off at our house and as I walk toward our front door, I see a bird standing in front of me on the grass. The bird doesn't move when I come close. Slowly bending my knees until they touch the ground, I look at the bird and see a small burr covering one of its eyes. I bring a forefinger near and parallel to its feet and the bird hops onto my finger.

Raising my hand slowly to my hair, the bird hops onto my head and doesn't move. I slowly stand and take baby steps as I walk to the front door, open it and enter our living room.

My mother is there to greet me. She sees the bird on my head and says, "You have a bird on your head."

I say, "It has something in its eye." I reach up with a level forefinger and the bird hops onto it. I lower my hand and gently remove the burr from its eye with a thumb and forefinger. Then I raise the bird back to the top of my head where it hops onto my hair again. My mother opens the front door and I slowly walk outside. The bird flies away.

1952

God makes a first appearance

We're putting on a Christmas play in second grade and I'm backstage, listening as my classmates perform. I've already acted in a scene. My parents are in the crowded auditorium, which is filled with other parents and elementary school students.

I know what's coming. We've had three rehearsals. As one of my classmates delivers his lines, I put the tips of my forefingers in my ears, anticipating what my parents will hear. My classmate says: "And then God spoke to the shepherd ...." If I didn't hear the word "God" spoken, maybe my parents wouldn't hear it either.

I had never heard God mentioned before at home or in school. I didn't want my parents to be upset.

Summer, 1953

Sam the monkey

During the summer before starting third grade, my family goes on a vacation to Mexico. I don't know any families in Croton that go on vacations in other countries so I don't tell my friends where we're going.

The day before we leave, my good friend Lawrence Miller and I ride our bikes to the Railroad Pond, which has become a lake. We ride while holding fishing rods. I have a can of worms in my bike basket.

It's a hot day in July so we walk to a shaded spot and cast our fishing lines into the lake.

I notice three bottles of coke tied together within reach in the water. I pull them out and untie them. They're cold and the caps are rusted.

Using a bottle opener in my pocket knife, I pry the cap off a bottle and after I drink most of it. Lawrence tells me, "You shouldn't have drunk the Coke. The cap was rusted. We don't know how long it was in the water. You could get sick and die."

I'm scared. I didn't know I could die from drinking rust. Should I tell my parents that I might die before we leave for Mexico? If I don't tell them, what if I die in Mexico? I decide to not tell them. I wait and wait and nothing happens.

The following morning, we fly to Mexico City where we stay for a few days. Then we fly in a small plane and land at a little airport somewhere near the Mexico border with Guatemala. We drive on a road that passes through thick jungle.

The old hotel where we stay has many tall flowering plants in a cobblestone courtyard. Outside the courtyard there is a large swimming pool with nothing in it but two bullfrogs and a few puddles of water. My brothers and I ride horses each day. The horses repeatedly gallop a few miles down a dirt road to a silver mine, where, unprompted, they rear and race back to the hotel.

My parents give their young sons freedom to roam the grounds of the hotel for an hour or two each day, by ourselves or together.

One morning, as I walk through the hotel lobby, the English-speaking concierge asks me if I've met Sam the monkey. I say no. He points outside to a path and says it will take me where I'll find Sam.

I walk for a while down the path and a few feet in front of where the jungle begins, I see a small monkey sitting on a wood perch. One end of a lightweight chain is tied to his collar. The other end is tied to the wood post beneath him.

Standing about eight feet away, I call to him. "Hello, Sam." He stares at me. I talk to him for a few minutes and then I return to the hotel.

The next day, I visit Sam again, stopping about four feet from him. I say hello and ask how he's doing. He leaps onto me from his perch, wraps his arms and legs tightly around my body and defecates on a front pocket of my pants. Then he jumps back to his perch and stares at me.

Confused and shocked by what Sam just did, I look at the left front pocket of my pants, which has monkey feces on it. I take a large leaf from a plant and try to wipe it off, but I only smear it.

I return to our hotel room. My mother greets me and asks if I'm having fun. I tell her, "Sam made BM on my pants pocket." She asks me, "Who is Sam?" I tell her, "Sam the monkey." She looks at my pants and tells me to go in the bathroom and take a shower. "Make sure you use soap to clean yourself really well," she says. I shower and put on clean clothes.

A few weeks later, in Acapulco, I feel sick and I stay in our hotel room. We fly to Mexico City and then to New York. Home at last in Croton, I'm ill and jaundiced. Our doctor makes a house call and tells me I have hepatitis. My first thought is that I got it from Sam the monkey.

During my six-week recovery, my parents lean a ladder against my bedroom window, and my friend, Lawrence, visits me after school each day, standing on the ladder, talking with me, helping me with his friendship while I recover. Six weeks later, I return to school.

1953, third grade

First Amendment

On a Wednesday during lunch in my elementary school cafeteria, the noise level from everyone having fun, talking and laughing between bites of food is a little louder than usual, but no one seems bothered by it except Mrs. Callahan, one of two cafeteria monitors. In a voice loud enough to be heard, she says, "May I have your attention? Please talk quietly so we can all hear each other, OK?" The noise level remains where it is. She tries again to quiet us but is unsuccessful.

Shouting breaks out between two boys sitting at nearby tables. The shouting intensifies. Both boys stand. One approaches the other and throws a punch, which leads to a brief flurry of punches before Mrs. Callahan steps in, separates them and directs each to tables that are far apart.

They do as they're told. Mrs. Callahan calls to the other cafeteria monitor, "Keep an eye on both of them. I'll get Mr. Alston." She leaves the cafeteria and returns with the school's principal, Mr. Alston. There is a rumor that he keeps a paddle in his office.

He stands in the cafeteria now with his arms crossed and waits for all talking to stop. It does. He says, "I've been told that you didn't listen to Mrs. Callahan when she said you need to talk quietly in the cafeteria so you can hear each other. When Mrs. Callahan tells you to do something, you're to do it immediately. If you don't, I'll ask her to bring you to my office. Talking in school is a privilege. When that privilege is not respected, there are consequences. There won't be any talking allowed by students in the cafeteria for the rest of today, tomorrow and Friday. You can resume talking quietly on Monday. The silence begins now.

Violators will be brought to me."

He tells Mrs. Callahan, "Bring the boys who were fighting to my office." He leaves, followed by Mrs. Callahan and the two boys.

The next day, Thursday, no one talks during lunch in the cafeteria. That evening, after dinner, I'm sitting at the kitchen table in our Croton house with my brother, Peter, and my father. Peter is studying for a test the following day on the Bill of Rights and my father is discussing the First Amendment with him.

I listen and learn about our guaranteed freedoms of speech, expression, the right to assemble and petition. I'm especially interested in freedom of speech. I ask my father, "Do kids have the same First Amendment rights as adults?"

He says we do, but adds, "There are some limits to freedom of speech. For example, you can't yell 'Fire!' in a movie theater, unless there really is a fire. People could get hurt trying to get out."

I ask, "But if a person isn't a danger to anyone else, say a kid, do they have a right to talk when they want to?"

"Not in a class," Peter says. "If a teacher is teaching, you can't talk any time you want because of the First Amendment. You have to wait until the teacher calls on you to talk."

"What about on a school playground or in a school cafeteria during lunch?"

"You should be able to talk and have fun in both places," my father says. Peter agrees. My father adds, "Just don't talk so loud that someone has to talk over you."

Friday, before school begins, I'm on the playground, talking with my friend, Leonard, who is small and thin, likes pretzels and is an outfielder when we play baseball at school.

I tell Leonard, "This is the last day of no talking during lunch in the cafeteria."

"We should be allowed to talk," he says.

I agree. I tell him, "I learned that the First Amendment gives us the right to talk in the cafeteria and on the playground. It's the First Amendment of the Bill of Rights. We can talk as long as we're not putting anyone in danger or talking so loudly that people can't hear each other."

Leonard asks, "Who told you about the First Amendment?"

"My father."

"It's for kids too?"

"Yes," I say. "But students can't talk in class unless their teacher calls on them to talk."

"And in the cafeteria?"

"We can talk as long as we're not too loud."

"You're sure?"

"I'm sure."

He smiles and says, "Freedom of speech."

At noon, Leonard and I carry our lunch trays to a cafeteria table, talking as we walk past dozens of elementary school kids eating in silence.

As we sit down, Mrs. Callahan walks quickly to us and says, "There's no talking at all during lunch in the cafeteria until Monday."

"We have a right to talk now," I say. "I learned about our First Amendment right, freedom of speech. My father told me it's a right, even for kids."

"Freedom of speech for students is a privilege, not a right," Mrs. Callahan says.

"No," I say, "it's in the Constitution. We have freedom of speech."

"If you both continue to talk," she warns, "I'll have to take you to Mr. Alston's office."

"We're talking quietly," I say. "We're not disturbing anyone else."

"Let's go," she says. Both of you, come with me."

"OK." I say, and I stand, but Leonard remains seated.

"Are you coming peacefully?" she asks him.

"No," he says

She calls to the other cafeteria monitor, "I'm taking them to Mr. Alston's office. I'll be back in a few minutes."

Leonard says, "I'm not going to the principal's office. I didn't do anything wrong."

"There's no talking allowed until Monday," Mrs. Callahan says.

"Freedom of speech," Leonard replies.

She picks him up from his chair and he shouts "Freedom of speech! Freedom of speech!" I follow them out of the cafeteria, where she puts him down, takes him by the arm and walks us to Mr. Alston's office. He's busy but leaves his office briefly and has us promise to do what the cafeteria monitors ask, or he'll call our parents and discuss the situation with them.

We promise to do what the monitors ask. We don't want him to call our parents. He returns to his office and we sit outside his closed door on a bench without talking until the lunch hour is over. Then we walk to our English class, talking every step of the way.

1953

A second theft

I'm playing with my friend, Steve, on a Saturday at his house. He shows me his collection of coins from the 1800s. They're in a pile on a small table. His mother calls to him and he leaves the room for a few minutes. While he's gone, I take a coin from the pile and put it in my pocket. When I get home and I'm alone, I look at the coin in my hand. It's from 1859. I love the feel of it.

My mother walks into the room and asks, "What do you have there, Scotty?" I tell her, "A coin from 1859." She asks, "Where did you get it?" I say, "I found it in the woods behind our house."

For two days, my coin and where I found it become a family story. We imagine someone during the Civil War walking near our house and accidentally dropping the coin in the woods.

Monday, after my father returns from working in New York City, Peter tells him that he was talking in school with his friend David, Steve's older brother, about the coin from 1859 that I found in the woods. David told him that Steve showed me his old coins a few days ago and was missing a coin from 1859.

My father tells me what Peter told him. I confess and he returns the coin to Steve's father. After that, no one in my family ever talks about my theft of Steve's coin. I'm thankful for that.

Summer, 1954

God's secular back door

My brothers and I attend the Jewish Community of Cortlandt in Croton to learn about the history of Jews, but God isn't prayed to or talked about directly.

Classes at what we call the JCC are taught by the parents of the kids who go there. Almost all of them live with their families on Mount Airy, in Croton, referred to by some people in town as "Red Hill." In the 1940s and 1950s, many artists, bohemians, anarchists, progressives, and socialists settled here.

There are rumors that some men in town are going to set fire to the JCC building on a specific night because they think it's run by communists. My father and a few other men spend the night in the JCC building, armed with rifles. They return home at dawn after nothing happens.

1954, fourth grade

Mrs. Simonson

Monday, the first day of school, students in my new class sit in rows behind desks, and our teacher introduces herself. "Hello," she says. "My name is Mrs. Simonson. Welcome to our fourth-grade class." She is so beautiful and kind and fun to be with, that three boys, George, Nick and I, fall in love with her before the first school day ends.

The following day, the three of us hurry to Mrs. Simonson's class and claim seats in the front row center of the classroom. We will sit in these seats for the rest of the school year, in love with Mrs. Simonson.

During the first week of school, we learn that in addition to being a teacher, she is an actor and has a husband. We're unhappy that she has a husband.

We try so hard to please Mrs. Simonson that we become outstanding students. We're always polite and attentive in class. During lunch one day, we discuss her husband and George says, "We need to get rid of him."

Nick asks, "Do you mean kill him?"

George says, "Maybe not kill him, but get rid of him." He's half joking but we all want him gone.

The school year ends the way it began – with the three of us in love with Mrs. Simonson.

We decide to have a surprise party for her at her house. We know where she lives.

After the last day of school ends, the three of us walk into town to the Grand Union and buy ice cream and four bottles of Coke. We walk to Mrs. Simonson's house and wait for her outside. It's a hot day and the ice cream begins to melt. We open three of the Cokes with an opener in Nick's Swiss Army knife.

The ice cream continues to melt and I suggest that we have some before it turns to mush. They agree. I pull the lid off the container and tip it so some of the ice cream that's soupy runs into my mouth. Nick and George do the same.

Mrs. Simonson arrives home in her car and is happy to see us. I close the lid on the ice cream container. She invites us into her home and we sit at her kitchen table while she pours and scoops the ice cream into four bowls and pours what's left of the three opened Cokes and the unopened one, into four glasses. She gives us spoons and joins us at the table. I'm in heaven.

We tell her we're going to miss her. She thanks us for the surprise party and tells us how much it means to her. She says she's going to miss us too.

When the bowls and glasses are empty, she asks if we would like her to drive us home. We all say yes.

I sit next to her on the front seat of her car. George and Nick sit in back. After she drops them off at their homes, she drives me to my house on West Mount Airy Road and slows to a stop. My heart races and I want to hug her goodbye, but I'm too little-boy shy to do that.

I thank h er and she thanks me for being wonderful. I step out of the car and we wave goodbye.

1955

A gift from Nanny

Not long after my grandmother, Nanny, dies in October, 1955, I'm taking recorder lessons at the Bennet Conservatory in Croton. Early one evening, for reasons I don't remember, my mother takes me to my teacher's house for my music lesson. She tells me she'll pick me up in forty-five minutes.

Before knocking on the front door with my recorder in hand, I hear the rich sounds of a stringed instrument coming from inside the house. I knock lightly. No one responds so I open the door and walk in. The living room is softly lit by two small lamps on side tables and a brighter overhead light and shade that hangs over a round dining table. On this table is a large mound of silver dollars, shining in the light of the overhead lamp.

I listen to the music being played upstairs and I look at the silver dollars. I'm enchanted. I call, "Hello?"

My recorder teacher comes down the stairs and greets me with a knowing smile. . "Hello, Scotty." She's carrying her viola and bow. She asks, "Did you like the sound of my viola?"

"Yes!"

She smiles. "I thought you would."

My mother uses the eight hundred dollars she inherits from her mother to buy her three sons musical instruments: a French horn for Peter, a viola for me and a clarinet for Clem.

I begin taking viola lessons at the Bennet Conservatory. I love the sound that I make with my viola. So does my first viola teacher,

Frederick, but he assumes I know how to read music. He's wrong about that and during one viola lesson, he becomes so impatient with my difficulty reading sheet music that he throws a slender book of song lyrics and notations at me and in a loud voice tells me to pay attention.

That night I dream I'm in a small boxing ring with Frederick at the Croton Boys Club. He's slow and unable to defend himself against the flurry of punches I throw at him.

I tell my parents about Frederick, and I get a different viola teacher who is gentle and patient. He teaches me how to read music.

1956, sixth grade

Behind the wallpaper

My mother decides to change our living room wallpaper. When the old wallpaper on one wall is peeled off, my father finds a dusty green blackboard underneath. My mother delights in exposing the blackboard on the wall and decides not to cover it up with new wallpaper.

We all sign our names with chalk on the board. I write Scotty Seldin. I sit under the blackboard and imagine that I'm the teacher, more than a hundred years ago, teaching ten or fifteen kids in a one-room schoolhouse.

My mother changes her mind about leaving the old blackboard exposed and it disappears again for many decades to come.

1956

In my mind's eye

Clem and I like to fish, sometimes together, sometimes separately. Our bond is tight, as it is with everyone in our family. It's summertime and we decide to fish by ourselves, in different places. With his fishing rod in hand, he rides his bike down West Mount Airy to the Railroad Pond, which has deep groves of trees that surround most of it. The Railroad Pond is about five miles from where we live.

I ride my bike down East Mount Airy, fishing rod in hand, to a lake about ten miles away. While fishing, my mind becomes as still as the lake I fish in.

Perhaps an hour passes when, in my mind's eye, I see Clem on top of a boulder, a few hundred yards around the Railroad Pond where we've fished together before. He's scared. There are several snakes on the ground around the boulder. What I see within is as real as the lake in front of me.

I grab my fishing rod and quickly ride and push my bike up East Mount Airy Road to our house on West Mount Airy. I tell my mother what I'd seen while fishing, and where Clem is. She doesn't hesitate or ask questions. We hurry to her car and she drives to the Railroad Pond where Clem went to fish. I run on a path around the lake and find Clem on top of a boulder with several snakes on the ground below. He's very happy to see me. I find space between snakes to climb up the boulder and help him come down safely. Following me, he walks his bike to our mother's car and puts the bike and his rod in the trunk.

On the drive home, no one asks me how I knew Clem was in trouble and where he was, but I'm amazed by what happened. The experience revealed to me that there is much more to existence than everyday life lets on.

In a birthday card I received from Clem for my sixty-fifth birthday, he lists the many special adventures we've had together. Among them is "Rescued by you at Railroad Pond when snakes surrounded me."

1957, seventh grade

It's in my DNA

Ryan is in my class. He lets his classmates know that he lifts weights and is learning how to wrestle. He and I both wear braces on our teeth.

After school one day. he asks me if I'm Jewish. I say, "Yes. Why do you want to know?" He says, "I'm Christian. The Jews killed Jesus Christ." I ask him how he knows that. He says "Everyone knows it."

"No," I say, "not everyone. I read it was the Roman emperor who ordered Christ killed."

"No," Ryan insists. "It was the Jews."

I ask, "Do you worship Jesus Christ?"

"Yes."

"When Jesus died, he was a Jew," I say, "not a Christian. You're worshiping a Jew when you worship Jesus Christ."

"You're twisting things around," he says, clenching his fists. "The Jews killed Christ." He challenges me to a fight the following day after school at the high school track. He's bigger and stronger than I am, but I say, "OK." Word spreads that tomorrow we're going to fight after school at the high school track.

At home that night, I tell my father about my situation with Ryan and that a lot of people will be there to watch. My father asks if it's too late to settle this peacefully. I say yes. He asks, "Do you want me to talk with the school principal tomorrow morning so he'll stop the fight from happening?"

I don't want to be seen as someone who can't handle his own problems and has to have his father protect him. I say, "No, I'm going to fight him."

"Well," he asks, "is he strong?"

I nod. "He's a wrestler."

My father advises, "Since he's a wrestler, he may try to put his arms around you from behind and take you down. If he does that, fall backwards and land on top of him."

After school, a crowd of about forty kids gather in a large circle at the high school track, leaving plenty of space in the middle for the fight.

Ryan is waiting for me inside the circle, which opens so I can enter it. I have no idea what I'm going to do. I walk toward him and stop about three feet away. He asks, "Are you ready to fight?"

I tell him, "Ryan, I've been thinking this over and maybe there's another way to work things out between us without fighting." He shakes his head no. I throw a hard left hand to his face, hitting him in his mouth. His braces cut into his lips, which bleed profusely. I turn and walk out of the circle, as if I'd won the fight. I don't look back and Ryan never talks to me again.

1960

My cousin Michael

My cousin Michael was eight years older than I and after he died, I learned that he had an IQ of 203. He was tall, handsome, sensitive, kind and schizophrenic.

As a teenager, he read books about Buddhism. I was drawn to him. When I was four, he walked with me to a nearby Sears and Roebuck in Brooklyn and bought a present for me, just because he wanted to.

Years later, after we moved to Croton-on-Hudson, Thanksgiving at our house was my favorite holiday. It was a joyful gathering of my extended family, with cousins, aunts and uncles. My mother prepared a delicious feast, there was a fire in the fireplace, a football game with cousins after we ate, a walk to Shenley Hill.

I'm ten years old. It's Thanksgiving and I'm standing with my father, Michael and Peter near the top of the gently sloping lawn in our back yard. My father points to where the lawn ends and the beginning of woods begin. He tells Michael, "If you go down to where the trees are, there's a hornets' nest on the ground, just in front of the trees. Make sure you don't accidently walk into it. The hornets will sting you."

My father returns to our house, and Michael walks to the hornets' nest. He gently shakes it and hornets swarm out and sting him. He runs back to us, laughing happily, and tells us, "Now I know what it feels like to be stung by hornets."

During the second half of the 1950s, Michael's schizophrenia worsens and he's in and out of mental institutions. He's given electroshock therapy and the last time I see him, when he visits us in Croton, he's gained weight.

At dusk, before my father drives him to the Croton train station, Michael and I shake hands goodbye and as I watch him walk with my father outside to our car, I know I'll never see him again.

January 28, 1960, the school bus drops me off at our house, and as I walk down the driveway, Clem hurries toward me and says, "Mom's been crying. I don't know what's wrong."

Inside the living room, my mother is wiping away tears with a tissue. She tells Clem and me that our cousin Michael died after falling from the roof of a building in Brooklyn.

I burst into tears and lock myself in the bathroom where I cry uncontrollably. My mother tries to comfort me from the other side of the bathroom door, but I won't come out. I cry like I've never cried before.

Maybe a half hour later, maybe an hour, my mother tells me through the locked door that she and my father are going to drive to Brooklyn to be with her sister, Michael's mother. I unlock the door and leave the bathroom.

In the living room, before they leave for Brooklyn, my mother tells Clem and me that they'll be back late that night and she's left dinner for us. They hug us goodbye and drive to Brooklyn.

Peter is in his first year at college. Clem and I eat our dinner downstairs and watch TV until it's time to go to sleep. Michael's death is too horrible to talk about. Clem goes to his bedroom, I go to mine, but I don't turn on the light. I sit on my bed and think about Michael.

His spirit form appears, about five feet in front of me, featureless, spectral. I know it's him. His presence is neither comforting nor frightening. It just is.

I don't talk with anyone in my family or anyone else about having seen Michael's spirit the night he died. It's 1960. I don't want to be thought of as crazy.

That spring, my mother gives me a book that was important to Michael: *The Teachings of the Compassionate Buddha.* Opposite the dog-eared page where he stopped reading, he had written in pencil: "Meditate – do not waste your life."

1960

While playing my viola

The year Michael died, my first year of high school, I play my viola in the school orchestra. The transition from elementary school directly to high school is difficult for me. No one knows that I'm grieving my cousin's death, and as an eighth grader, I'm of little interest to most of the students in high school, who are taller, stronger and more mature than I am.

For the first time in my life, I become depressed, but I don't realize it until the director of the school orchestra asks Peter Salaff to sit next to me and play a page of music that the orchestra is working on. Peter is an extraordinary violinist who would go on to teach music at a university and play violin with the Cleveland String Quartet.

Sitting next to him as he plays his violin and I play my viola, the music he creates is so breathtakingly beautiful that I cry for the five minutes that he plays sitting next to me.

October, 1962

The Cuban Missile Crisis

After a failed U.S. attempt to overthrow the government of Fidel Castro in Cuba, United States surveillance photographs show missile silos under construction in Cuba. U.S. intelligence implicates the Soviet Union, and it is determined that the silos are being constructed for medium-range and intermediate-range ballistic missiles.

President John Kennedy imposes a blockade of Cuba and sends warships to the region to enforce it. He vows to not let any Soviet ships get past U.S. battleships. The fate of the world is solely in the hands of two men: John Kennedy and Nikita Krushchev.

For five terrifying days, Soviet Union ships steam toward Cuba with missiles reported to be hidden under very large tarps on the decks of several ships.

For five days, a catastrophic nuclear war between the two nuclear superpowers seems likely. Everything living is threatened with extinction. I'm terrified, as is everyone else who knows what's happening.

At the last possible moment, Soviet ships veer off a collision course. They turn around and return to a Russian port.

Shock waves reverberate globally from how close the world came to a deadly nuclear winter.

Six weeks later, I'm sitting at a school desk in Dr. Graham's twelfth grade political science class. The school's air raid siren wails, and everyone knows the drill. Stand and wait to be led, single file, past a long glass wall to the gymnasium, where we sit on the floor until we hear the all clear, after which we return to class.

I had participated in several high school air raid drills in the past, but my still-raw trauma from the Cuban Missile Crisis expresses itself.

I turn to my friend Barbara, who stands next to me in class, and tell her, "I'm not going to participate. This is insane — sitting on a gym floor to protect us from a nuclear war."

"It *is* insane," Barbara says. "I'm not going to participate either."

All the other students leave the room and walk to the gym. Dr. Graham stands near the open classroom door and motions for us to leave. We approach him and I say, "We're not going to participate."

He asks Barbara, "You too?"

"Yes."

"Then you both need to talk about this with the principal, Dr. Anderson."

We walk to Dr. Anderson's office and tell him we're not going to take part in the air raid drill.

He tells us, "Student participation in air raid drills is not optional. If you refuse, you will be suspended from school until you promise to take part in the next air raid drill."

We're resolute and he suspends us from school. We walk to Barbara's house in town and she asks if I've heard of a singer, Bob Dylan. I haven't. She says, "He has his first album out. Would you like to hear it?"

I say yes and we listen to *Bob Dylan.* My connection to his voice and songs is immediate and deep.

We stay out of school for a few days and when we return, we tell Dr. Anderson that we'll take part in the next air raid drill. There are only about six more months until we graduate. We figure there won't be another air raid drill before the school year ends, and we're right.

When we return to school, we have to make up the time and assignments we missed while we were suspended. My first day back, after class hours, I'm sitting at a desk in Mr. Jansen's chemistry classroom, reading assigned pages in my chemistry book. He's writing with chalk on the blackboard.

A very popular novel at the time is *Lord of the Flies* by William Golding. In one scene, a group of boys surround a classmate and chant at him, "Kill the pig! Cut his throat! Kill the pig! Bash him in!"[1]

As I sit in Mr. Jansen's classroom, four high school students walk into the room and stand in front of me. They chant, "Kill the pig! Kill the pig! Kill the pig! Kill the pig!" Mr. Jansen looks at them and they leave. Then he turns back to writing on the blackboard.

An hour later, I leave the classroom and the school, crying as I run down the grass hillside to the street.

Over the winter of 1962 – '63, in the aftermath of the Cuban Missile Crisis, Bob Dylan writes "Masters of War," which begins:

"Come you masters of war
You that build all the guns
You that build the death planes
You that build the big bombs
You that hide behind walls
You that hide behind desks
I just want you to know
I can see through your masks"[2]

Late May, 1963

Has anyone seen Scott?

About three weeks before my high school graduation, I'm in Washington, D.C. at the Smithsonian Museum on a senior class trip. We've spent an hour and a half at the museum, and we're scheduled to leave soon.

Mr. Brooks, one of two trip chaperones, gathers our class on the first floor of the museum. He stands next to Mrs. Aubrey, the other chaperone, and says, "Everyone is to be on the bus by 2:00 o'clock. That's in twenty minutes, so if you have to use the bathroom or see one last exhibit, do that now. Mrs. Aubrey will stay here and at 1:55, she'll walk to the bus with any of you who are still in the museum." He leaves the building and I consider leaving also.

Ever since Barbara and I didn't take part in the high school air raid drill and were suspended, several of my classmates with whom I'd been friends since kindergarten have avoided me. I return to the bus.

As I walk past the bus driver and continue toward Mr. Brooks, who sits half way back in an aisle seat, I glance at the carry-on zippered bags that line the bus luggage racks, extending from the front of the bus to the rear, on both sides of the aisle. The racks have depth. I get an idea.

I stop and stand next to Mr. Brooks. "Back early," he says.

I nod. "I have an unusual request."

"What is it?"

"As an experiment, would you let me hide on a luggage rack behind some luggage, and would you pretend that you don't know where I am when everyone returns to the bus?"

He smiles. "Why would you want to do that?"

"Have you ever wondered what people really think of you?"

"Yes. "

"Well, here's my chance to find out what my classmates think of me. After everyone's back on the bus at 2:00, would you wait a few minutes for me to arrive? Then, when I don't show up, ask everyone if we should wait any longer for me to return."

He says, "OK, as long as it doesn't delay our trip more than five minutes."

"It won't," I assure him.

All the students and Mrs. Aubrey are back on the bus at 2:00. Mr. Brooks checks his watch and asks, "Has anyone seen Scott?"

Someone says, "He left the Smithsonian a few minutes after you did."

Two minutes pass and Mr. Brooks asks the group, "Should we wait for Scott any longer, or should we leave?"

Someone says, "It's hot, let's go." It's Nolan. I listen, stretched out on the luggage rack near the left-rear of the bus, unseen behind carry-on bags. Someone else says, "Yeah, let's go." It's Lana. I recognize her voice. Someone says "No, wait for him." It's Lawrence. Someone else says, "He'll be here soon." It's Ritchie. "We should wait for him." It's Ruth.

I climb down from the luggage rack to a few groans. The bus heads toward the Lincoln Memorial.

"Why were you up there?" someone asks as I take a seat.

I shrug. "Everyone has to be somewhere."

Fall, 1963

Is it dangerous? Do you carry a gun?

When I begin my freshman year at American University in Washington, D.C., I bring my viola with me and I audition for the university orchestra, which will provide music for a theater production of "Ahmed and the Night Visitors." My audition is successful. I go to my first rehearsal and discover that there are numerous viola solos in the score. The auditorium is large. After the first rehearsal, I become nervous about playing solo in front of seven or eight hundred people.

I go to see the director of the production and tell him, "I won't be able to play viola in the show."

He asks me why and I make up an answer on the spot. "I just got a part-time job as a detective in Chevy Chase, Maryland."

He knows I'm lying. He asks, "Have you worked as a detective before?"

"No."

He presses me. "We were counting on you. We don't have another student who plays viola."

"I'm sorry," I say. "I wish I could continue, but I need this job."

He asks, "Is it dangerous? Do you carry a gun?"

"No," I say. "I just follow people, take notes, see where they go and what they do."

He's had enough. "Sorry you won't be in the show," he says, and he walks away.

Over the following decades, wherever I'm living, I keep my viola in its case on the floor of a closet or under a chest of drawers. I play it occasionally and it remains dear to me, though it falls into some disrepair at the end of the twentieth century.

Spring and summer, 1964

If a Jew came to my home in Syria, I would kill him

Rummaging through some stored papers recently, I came upon a review of Jack Kerouac's book, *On the Road*, that I had written in 1964 for a spring semester freshman writing class at American University. Reading the paper again, I saw its relevance to understanding the story I am about to share with you. In my review, I wrote: "Kerouac's book relates stories of endless wild drives across the United States. He speaks of an obsessive restlessness which drives these forerunners of the Beat Generation to hitching anywhere and everywhere, searching for kicks and truth, stealing and wrecking cars, picking up girls with wild abandon, making love to them and moving on, never stopping."

The final paragraph of my paper concludes: "Just reading Kerouac's *On the Road* is like just reading a review of a play without ever seeing the play. Such vicarious satisfactions seem to be more than enough for most people today. This is unfortunate. Plays must be seen as well as reviewed, and *On the Road* must be lived as well as read. If nothing else, this is the meaning of Kerouac."

I received an A for the paper and there was a one-word comment from Professor Yarnell: "Beware."

During spring semester, 1964, I see a flyer on a campus bulletin board at American University for a cheap roundtrip summer flight to London. I worked the previous summer in New York City as an office boy at an advertising agency and saved enough money to go abroad. I buy a roundtrip ticket to London.

From London, I travel to Paris and then to Grenoble, France. I want to experience a culture unlike the one that has imprinted itself on me with everything American, including how I think and what I think about. I want to spend time in an entirely different culture.

In Grenoble, I carry my suitcase to the highway and start hitchhiking south through France, then south again through Spain to Algeciras, where I board a small ship that travels to Tangier, Morocco.

I stay at The African Hotel and spend a week walking the streets of Tangier, excited to be where everything and everyone is different.

There are men wearing long white djellabas and fezzes, and marketplaces with vendors selling parrots, frying pans, gems, tools, pigeons, Berber blankets, live chickens, hats, sweaters, shoes, you name it, someone's selling it.

I hear a mix of different languages spoken; atonal Moroccan music coming from houses; a call to prayer from a mosque, five times a day.

Exploring the narrow streets of the Casbah, I see a woman holding a snake while a young boy bangs on a drum.

Each day I see a man in a turban who sits on a blanket with his back against the wall of a building in the Casbah. He has a large pile of live snails in front of him, and every ten or fifteen minutes he puts his hand in a large bowl of water and sprinkles some on the snails. If one of them crawls out of the pile, he stands, walks to the wandering snail, lifts it off the concrete and gently returns it to the pile.

I imagine him selling snails from a pile of live snails on Fifth Avenue in front of the Forty-second Street Library. How long would the New York police let him sell his snails there? In the Casbah of Tangier, he's allowed to sell his snails without paying rent or having a "Snail Salesman" business card. He has no need to call this corner of the Casbah his office.

One day at a cafe, I meet three Moroccan men who ask me to join them at their table. I do so. They're an upbeat, fun-to-be-with group, and they all speak English. I tell them I'm American and they smile. I wonder what they're smiling about.

They ask about my life in America and I tell them I'm a college student from New York. I ask about their lives in Morocco and they say they're school teachers with the summer off. Before they leave the café, one of them asks me, "Would you like to see a caravan that's crossing the desert and will arrive tomorrow afternoon at four o'clock?" I say yes. He writes an address on a piece of paper, hands it to me, and tells me how to get there.

The following day, I arrive a few minutes early at the address I was given the day before. I peer into the distance but I don't see a caravan coming. I wait fifteen or twenty minutes when the three men from the café appear and walk up to me, laughing good naturedly.

One of them asks, "The caravan hasn't arrived yet?"

"No," I say.

He grins and says, "Only an American would think that a caravan crossing the desert would arrive in Tangier this afternoon at four o'clock."

We all laugh and I realize how culturally conditioned I am by the American way of life and time.

The following day, I'm walking through Tangier. A boy, maybe ten years old, approaches me and asks, "Hey mister, do you want my sister?"

"Your sister?"

"Yes. Do you want her?"

"No thanks."

He asks, "Do you want my brother?"

"No," I say, and I continue walking.

I'm beginning to feel lonely and I decide to leave Tangier. I take a train across Morocco to Fes, spend two days there, then another train to Oujda, where I get a visa to enter Algeria. I feel a need to keep traveling.

The next day, mid-afternoon, I board a train that crosses into Algeria, scheduled to arrive at midnight in Algiers. I'm not sure why I'm going there.

Sidestepping my way through the train's narrow aisle with my suitcase, I find an empty seat in the train's last car. Seated, I watch three men and two goats watch me. My loneliness deepens. I miss my family and friends.

Looking out the window, I see miles of empty fields pass by, then a few donkeys, dogs, children and mothers in front of small houses, with men farming the earth.

About an hour before midnight, I carry my suitcase to the train's dining car. I'm uneasy about arriving in Algiers at midnight. I don't know where I'm going to stay.

I order a beer. The bartender shakes his head when I hand him Moroccan dirhams. He shows me an Algerian bill and says, "Dinar."

I'm about to give the beer back when a man standing nearby steps forward and pays for my beer with Dinar. Speaking English, he says, "My name is Ahmad." He holds an open bottle of beer in his hand.

"Thanks for the beer," I say. "My name is Scott." We shake hands.

"Where are you from?" he asks.

"America."

"Traveling alone? "

"Yes."

"What brings you to Algeria?"

"I was hitchhiking through France and Spain and I wanted to see North Africa. Are you Algerian?"

"No," he says, "Syrian. I'm a translator for the Syrian army. I'll be visiting a Syrian friend who is in Algiers for a few days."

I drink my beer and look at my watch. I ask, "Will you be staying at a hotel tonight?"

"Yes."

"Can I go with you and get a room there? I've never been to Algiers before."

"Yes, of course," he says. We make small talk for a few minutes and then he asks, "Do you like your President Johnson?"

I'm surprised by his question. "I don't know," I say. "It's less than a year since he was elected."

"I dislike him," Ahmad says. "He helped the Jews in Israel. Did you know that?"

"No."

"The Jews killed my brother in the war."

"I'm so sorry."

"The Israelis think the war is over. It isn't."

I change the subject and talk about my life growing up in New York with my family. I ask about his family, and he talks about his early years in Damascus.

We share a taxi from the Algiers train station to l'Hotel Afrique, and as Ahmad talks in French to the concierge, I say to him, "I'd like a room by myself."

They talk and Ahmad tells me, "There aren't any rooms available now, but he says my room has two beds. If you want, you can sleep in one of them."

I'm disturbed by what he said about Jews, but where am I going to go at this hour? I'm exhausted. I say, "O.K. Thanks."

We carry our suitcases up a flight of stairs and down a hallway. Ahmad stops in front of a hotel door and says, "We're in here." He unlocks the door and turns on an overhead light as we enter the room. We each place our suitcase near one of the two parallel single beds that are about four feet apart.

He uses the bathroom, then I do. When I come out, the overhead light is off and Ahmad is in bed. The room is dimly lit by moonlight.

I take off my shoes and get into bed, wondering if he knows I'm a Jew. When I applied for my passport and was asked my religion on the application, I wrote "Judaism." I decide to leave the hotel before he's awake in the morning, but I don't know how I'm going to manage with only Moroccan money.

At dawn, after a few hours of sleep, I put on my shoes, and as I carry my suitcase toward the door, Ahmad awakens and sits up in bed. "Where are you going?"

I stop and face him. "I'm leaving Algiers today for Marseille."

"No, no," he says, getting out of bed. "You haven't seen Algiers yet. I'll show you around the city. Leave your suitcase here."

I don't know what to do. I put my suitcase down. He gets dressed and we leave the room. My passport and wallet are in my pockets.

As we walk the streets, Ahmad talks about the city of Algiers and the Algerian war with France that ended two years ago. He points out the buildings that still have bullet holes in the walls.

I ask why there are soldiers on so many street corners carrying guns. He says they protect the safety of Algerians.

Mid-morning, we stop at a bank and I exchange my Moroccan dirham for Algerian dinar. Ahmad makes a phone call from the bank and we have lunch in a café with Emir, Ahmad's Syrian friend. I never learn why they are in Algeria.

That evening we meet with Emir again for dinner at a restaurant. After a second round of beers, their talk turns to Jews. I listen to their comments, which seem intended to goad me into a response.

"Someday I will fill a bottle with Jewish blood and drink."

"Hitler is my idol. I worship him."

"President Kennedy was killed by a Jewish conspiracy."

"There will be war and the Arabs will push and burn the Jews into the sea."

Ahmad looks at me and says, "If a Jew came to my home in Syria, I would kill him." He asks, "If you travel to Syria, will you come to my home?"

"No," I say, "I wouldn't. As you apparently know, I'm a Jew. I wouldn't want you to kill me."

"We know you are a Jew," he says, "and we know you are a spy for Israeli Intelligence."

I'm staggered. I tell him, "I'm not a spy. I'm a college student."

He's certain. "College students don't travel to Algeria. You ask questions about soldiers on the streets so you can give information to Israeli intelligence."

Their hatred for Jews is more powerful than anything I've ever experienced. We leave the restaurant. Ahmad says goodbye to Emir, who says he'll stop by our hotel tomorrow morning.

As Ahmad and I walk back to L'Hotel Afrique, he tells me, "If you're thinking of running away, don't. People know you're here."

I'm terrified. I realize that if they kill me, no one in my family will ever know where and how I died.

We walk in silence to the hotel and return to the room we still share. While Ahmad is in the bathroom, I take a bread knife from my suitcase and slip it under my bed's pillow.

When he leaves the bathroom, I enter it and close the door behind me. I wash my face, brush my teeth and try to calm myself.

The lights are off when I reenter the room. I take off my shoes and get into bed.

We face each other in the parallel beds. I grip my bread knife. All night I wait, expecting him to attack.

Finally, dawn. I pack my suitcase. Ahmad sits up in bed. "You're leaving?" he says.

"Yes, for Marseille. Will you help me get to the port?"

"Yes," he says.

We take a taxi to the port and he leads me to a ship that will be going to Marseille.

A group of about a hundred men are waiting to buy tickets. We stand behind them and Ahmad talks with a man in uniform and learns that the ship is scheduled to leave in an hour and a half and most of the available tickets for today have been sold.

I ask him, "Will I be able to buy a ticket for today's ship to Marseille?"

He shrugs. "Maybe not."

I panic and push my way through the crowd, ignoring hands that roughly grab at me, trying to stop me, but they can't because adrenaline powers me forward. I reach the ticket seller's window and push money toward the man selling tickets. I shout, "Billet! Billet! Marseille!" He takes my money and gives me a ticket and change. I turn to leave and I'm pushed hard and out of the crowd by several men.

Ahmad approaches me. "So," he says, "you have a ticket. "You escape with your life."

"Thank you for helping me leave."

"War will come with Israel," he replies. "Perhaps we'll meet again."

We shake hands and I board the ship that will take me to Marseille.

I'm shaken to my soul.

1965

The Vietnam War becomes America's war

I'm a junior at American University.

March, 1965, President Lyndon Johnson orders an increase in the number of U.S. combat troops in Vietnam from 5500 Marines to 50,00 ground troops.

At an anti-war march not far from the United States Capitol, I wait to join the Washington, D.C. contingent as each state's group of protesters pass by, walking behind someone holding a sign with their state's name on it. There are between fifteen and fifty people marching in each group.

As about twenty protesters from the Ohio contingent pass by, I see my brother, Peter, marching with them. I call to him. He turns, we both smile, hurry toward each other and hug. Then he runs back to his Ohio group and continues marching with them. I wait and join the Washington D.C. protesters.

I'm actively opposed to American involvement in Vietnam's civil war. I meet regularly with three other students at American University to organize anti-war protests on campus. At first, only ten to fifteen students show up and demonstrate with us, but the number grows as the number of Americans coming home in wheelchairs or body bags grows.

By 1966, U.S. troop levels have risen to 400,000, with thousands of Americans and Vietnamese killed and injured each week. By 1967, most U.S. males my age are wondering if they will be drafted and sent to Vietnam.

I go through the motions of being a student, taking exams and reading books, but my mind, time and effort are focused on protesting the war in Vietnam.

1967

The theft of everything I own

At the start of my senior year at American University, I rent a partially furnished, ground-level studio apartment in Washington D.C. It comes with a brown couch, a brown easy chair, a single bed and a fully equipped kitchen.

When I move in, I bring everything I own: a stereo, speakers, about thirty records, a small bookshelf full of books, my clothes and shoes, a warm wool hat, a summer cap, a Mexican blanket and a four-foot-long poster of Charlie Chaplin, which I tape to the apartment wall that faces the front door.

My neighbor lives in an apartment with a front door to the left of mine. Our two apartments are connected units, separate from a row of apartments behind us, which are farther back from the street. My neighbor's front door has a peephole. Mine does not. I hear people coming and going at odd hours and I wonder if whoever lives there is a drug dealer.

I don't meet my neighbor until early afternoon of the day when everything in my apartment that I own is stolen, except the Charlie Chaplin poster.

Early that morning, as I'm about to leave my apartment at 7:45 and drive to American University for a 9 o'clock class, I can't find my apartment key. I search everywhere but it's missing.

I try to remember when I last had the key. I think back to what I did the day before, after my second class. I shopped at a supermarket and bought food and drink for the week, then drove home and carried two full bags to my front door. I held both bags with one arm, and with my left hand, I took my apartment key from a pants pocket and opened the front door. I brought the two bags inside and closed the door behind me. "Oh no!" I say out loud when I realize I left my key in the front door. I check and it's not there.

I don't want to be late for class. I leave, closing the front door behind me, and drive to American University. Early afternoon, I return to my apartment and open the front door. There's nothing of mine inside, except my poster of Charlie Chaplin on the wall in front of me.

I knock on my neighbor's door. No answer. I knock harder. The door opens. He's half asleep and looks like he hasn't shaved in four or five days. "Hi," I say, "I'm your neighbor, Scott."

"Luke," he says.

I tell him, "Someone stole everything I own from my apartment. I accidentally left my apartment key in my front door yesterday afternoon. When I came home carrying two bags of groceries, I forgot to take the key out of the front door lock. Someone must have taken the key and come back this morning to steal my stuff."

Luke looks stoned. He shrugs. "I don't know anything about it."

I tell him, "I think the person who stole from me knows you and was coming to see you yesterday when he saw my key in the door and took it."

"Nobody came to see me yesterday," Luke says, "and no one's come to see me today. I've been away since I left at nine this morning. I got back about a half hour before you knocked on my door."

"I need your help."

"Hey — I don't know anything about this."

I'm matter of fact. "I'm going to call the cops. They'll come and write a crime report. They'll see that your door is next to mine and they'll ask me who lives there. They may knock on your door to talk with you. I don't care how you make a living. I'm not going to say anything about you. All I'm interested in is getting my stuff back as soon as possible. After that happens, I'll call the police and tell them that while I was out, everything stolen was returned to my apartment."

Luke isn't ready to help yet, but I can see that he's considering it. I add, "You don't want the police coming around asking questions. We both know why."

He bristles. "You don't know anything about me, so back off."

"Do you know who robbed me?"

"No."

"Do you know anyone who may have heard about the robbery?"

He pauses. "You'll keep me out of this?"

"Yes. You have my word."

"You know Charlie's in Georgetown?"

"The food and dance place?"

He nods. "Ask for Frenchy, one of the owners. He has his ear to the ground. He may have heard something."

"Thanks."

I call the closest police department. A half hour later, a patrol car stops in front of my apartment. A policeman gets out and I tell him about the robbery. He writes a brief report and leaves.

It's the middle of the afternoon. I call my friend Joe and tell him about the robbery and about going to talk with Frenchy at Charlie's in Georgetown. I ask if he'll help me get my stuff back that night. He says yes.

Early evening, I drive to Joe's apartment and he follows me in his car to Georgetown. We park near Charlie's and walk in. It's crowded and alive with Friday night energy, mostly college students eating burgers and fries. A few couples dance near a jukebox playing Fats Domino.

I ask someone if he knows Frenchy. He points to a tall man with blonde hair tied back in a pony tail.

Joe and I approach Frenchy and introduce ourselves. I tell him, "Luke said you might have heard about a robbery that happened today."

"Yeah," Frenchy says. "He called and said you'd probably stop by. He said you called the cops."

"I did. A cop came and wrote a report. I don't want anyone to go to jail for this. I just want my stuff back. When I get it back, I'll tell the cops everything was returned to my apartment while I was out."

"That's what you'd have to do," Frenchy says.

"That's what I *will* do," I say. "Have you heard anything about the robbery?"

"Maybe." He sizes us up. "Swear on your life you'll keep me and Luke out of this."

Joe and I promise we will. Frenchy writes an address on a piece of paper and hands it to me. He says, "Tell R.T. you're looking for a room to rent."

"Thanks," I say. "We were never here."

We drive our cars to the address Frenchy gave me, near Dupont Circle. I park in front of a two-story house. Joe parks behind me.

We walk to the front door, and I ring the doorbell. The door opens and a man with bushy black hair stands in front of us. He's wearing my lightweight green sweater. He asks, "What do you want?"

I hear Paul McCartney singing "Eleanor Rigby." I have *Revolver*, the album the song is on. I say, "My name is Willie. I'm a student at George Washington University, looking for a room to rent near Dupont Circle. A guy I met there suggested I check here."

"Who was that?"

"Someone named John." I figure most people know someone named John.

"Tall guy with glasses?"

"Yeah."

"I'm R.T."

We shake hands.

I turn to Joe and tell R.T., "This is my friend, Carl." They shake hands.

"Come on in," he says. "There isn't a room available now, but there may be in a few weeks." He leads us into the living room.

As we walk in, I see two men and two women sitting on a rug, laughing, passing a joint, listening to *Revolver*. I nod to Joe and he nods back.

We walk toward a stairway. On a table, I see my stereo and speakers, now playing "I'm Only Sleeping." To the left of the table, I see my bookcase, filled with books.

At the top of the stairs, R.T. tells us, "There are three bedrooms up here." We pass two closed doors and he stops in front of the third door. "This room is the one that may be available to rent in about three weeks." He knocks on the door. No one answers. "We can't go in, but you can take a look from the hallway." He opens the door and hallway light shines into the room. My Mexican blanket covers a bed.

We return to the living room. I walk to my stereo and lift the needle from the turntable.

"Hey!" R.T. shouts. "What are you doing?" Everyone looks at me.

I face R.T. "You know the stuff you stole today? It's mine. I've come to get it all back."

He pulls a switch blade from a back pocket and the blade springs open. "Leave before I hurt you," he says, holding the blade in front of me.

"Put your knife away," I say. "We have a friend who lives near Dupont Circle. If I don't stop by sometime in the next hour, he's going to call the cops and have them come looking for us here. I want you to help us carry everything that's mine to my car and Carl's. Once that's done, you won't have to worry about being busted. I made a police report but after I get my stuff back, I'll call the police and say that while I was out, everything was returned."

R.T. closes his switch blade and puts it in a pants pocket. He says, "You know what will happen to you if you don't call off the police."

"Yes," I say, "I know."

"If anyone gets busted, we'll find you."

"Understood. You can get things rolling by giving me the key to my front door and the sweater you're wearing. Then you can get my Mexican blanket from the room we looked in."

R.T. reaches into a front pocket and hands me my key. He takes off my sweater and gives it to me. I put on the sweater. He walks upstairs. Joe and I take my stereo and speakers to my car and put them on the back seat. R.T. approaches and hands my Mexican blanket to me. I put it on the passenger side of my car's front seat.

Shuttling back and forth from the house to our cars, Joe and I make three stacks of my record albums on the back seat and the floorboards of my car. We put my books in a large plastic garbage bag that R.T. gives us and Joe places it on the back seat of his car. We slide my bookcase into the opened trunk of his car and use some cord to secure the trunk to the license plate because the bookcase sticks out.

In the living room, I ask R.T., "Where are the rest of my clothes?"

"In my room," he says. "I'll put everything in large plastic bags."

"Let's do it," I say.

He gets the bags and I follow him into his room. He opens the closet door and the top drawer of a chest of drawers. I watch him fill three garbage bags with my sports jacket, sweaters, underwear, hats, socks, pants, shirts, one tie, a winter coat and white sneakers. We each carry a bag to Joe's car and place them on the back seat and floorboards.

Standing in front of our cars, I tell R.T., "I'll call the police department tomorrow afternoon and say that all my stolen stuff was returned while I was out in the morning."

We shake hands and he returns to his house. Joe and I drive to my apartment, and two hours later, everything is back where it was before it was stolen. I thank Joe, who drives home. It's past midnight when I get into bed, kept warm by my Mexican blanket.

The following afternoon, I call the police department and tell an officer that while I was out in the morning, everything stolen was returned to my apartment.

"Is that your story?" the policeman asks.

"That's my story," I tell him.

August 3, 1968

The Tombs

I graduate from American University, and late summer, 1967, I enroll in graduate school at C.W.Post College on Long Island for fall semester. While there, I help organize anti-war protests with other students.

August 3, 1968, I take a train from Long Island to Manhattan to join an anti-war protest in front of the armory on 28th Street and Lexington Avenue. I'm feeling lonely. I was going to go to the demonstration with two students, but they didn't show up at the train station before I left.

When I arrive, a crowd of about two hundred people are in front of the armory, chanting "End the war in Vietnam!" I join them, standing in front of a car parked in a long line of other parked cars on the block.

The chanting becomes more impassioned and demanding: "End the war in Vietnam! End the war in Vietnam!" Then "Peace now! Peace now!"

We demonstrate loudly and peacefully for about an hour when five mounted policemen ride horses toward the crowd, shouting, "Clear the street!" "Clear the street!" Policemen on foot appear. Holding batons, they walk toward the demonstrators.

A policeman rides his horse at the protesters where I'm standing, in front of a car. To avoid getting hurt by the charging horse, I climb on top of the car in back of me. A young man in a soldier's uniform, who had been chanting next to me, climbs on top of the car I'm on, for the same reason.

The horse barrels past us and a policeman on foot steps up to the car we're standing on and shouts, "Get off the car!" I drop to my knees and slide backwards off the car, as does the man in the soldier's uniform.

The policeman grabs me. I break his grip and run up a side street. He chases me. I look over my shoulder as he closes in. I stop, turn around, face him and say, "If you're going to arrest me, I'm not resisting arrest." He says, "You're under arrest. Put your hands behind your back." He handcuffs me, pats me down and leads me to a police van with its rear doors open.

I step into the van and join six other handcuffed demonstrators who sit on two benches that line both sides of the van.

Handcuffed, the man in the soldier uniform is thrown head first into the van, followed by his arresting officer, who closes the van doors and beats this man repeatedly on the floor. We're driven to a police precinct. The van doors open and seven of us step out.

The man in the soldier uniform is carried out of the van, unconscious, and the arresting officer drags him by his feet up the concrete steps of the precinct.

In the precinct, the policeman who arrested me says, "You have the right to remain silent. Anything you say can be used against you in a court of law."

He asks for my name, address, and date of birth. I give him the information and ask if he'll remove the handcuffs because they're cutting into my wrists. He does so. He says, "You've been charged with the following criminal offenses: inciting to riot, felonious assault, reckless endangerment. resisting arrest and disorderly conduct."

"What?" I say. "I didn't do any of that."

"Would you like to write a response to the charges?"

"No. I want to remain silent until I get a lawyer. Where will I be taken from here?"

"You'll be arraigned at Manhattan Criminal Courts, 100 Centre Street, then held at the Manhattan Detention Complex nearby, at 125 White Street."

"The Tombs?"

"Yes."

I've read about the Tombs in New York newspapers. It's the worst jail in the city, notorious for violence. "I'd like to make a phone call," I say.

He points to a phone on a desk. I call my father and tell him I've been arrested, where I am, that I'm innocent and will soon be taken to Manhattan Criminal Courts, 100 Centre Street, for arraignment.

He asks, "After your arraignment, where will you be taken?"

"Manhattan Detention Complex, 125 White Street. It's close to the

Manhattan Criminal Courts building."

He tells me he'll drive to the city and get me out.

I'm handcuffed again and led to a police car where I sit in the back seat between two policemen, one of whom arrested me. Two policemen sit in front. One of them drives the patrol car south toward the Manhattan Criminal Courts building.

The arresting policeman, sitting to my left, tells the other three, "This guy is charged with inciting to riot, felonious assault, reckless endangerment, resisting arrest and disorderly conduct. What should do with him?"

The policeman sitting next to the driver says, "I think we should beat him up and throw him in the East River."

The arresting policeman says, "I'm in."

I don't say anything. I'm scared. I don't know what they're going to do. After driving south another mile or so, the driver turns off the road onto a clearing and stops the car, overlooking the East River. He turns off the engine, looks at his watch and says, "We're running late." The policeman to my right says, "Let's get to the arraignments."

I quietly say, "If you don't mind, I'd like to break the tie and vote to go to the arraignments." One of the policemen chuckles and says, "Let's go."

At my arraignment, I stand before a judge who reads the charges against me. He asks how I plead. I tell him "Not guilty." He asks what I do, how long I've lived in New York State, and who is coming to get me. I answer his questions. I'm handcuffed again and walked to the Tombs.

In the Tombs, aptly named, I'm led down a windowless, dimly lit, dank hall, past cells with detainees, to an unoccupied cell where my handcuffs are removed and I'm locked inside.

The cell has a cot with an army blanket on it, a turn of the century toilet and sink and a grimy concrete floor.

Four hours later, I'm released from my cell. My wallet and keys are returned to me, and I leave the Tombs. Outside, I see my father waiting for me. As he drives us north, I tell him about the anti-war protest and my arrest.

Late evening, we arrive at our family home in Croton-on-Hudson. My parents are shelter from the storm.

Four months later, my father meets me at Manhattan Criminal Courts for a scheduled pretrial hearing. I have a lawyer representing me. The arresting officer doesn't show and the hearing is postponed.

Three months later, a second scheduled pretrial hearing is postponed because the arresting officer doesn't appear in court. Again, my father and lawyer are there.

At my third scheduled pretrial hearing, the judge stands behind a desk with his chair behind him. At the other two postponed pretrial hearings, the judges were seated.

As I wait with my father and lawyer for my docket to be called, I notice that the judge has winced several times.

Two dockets before mine is called, an arresting officer doesn't appear in court for a pretrial hearing. The judge postpones the hearing with a warning that if arresting officers don't appear in court, there will be consequences.

When the docket before mine is called, again the arresting officer doesn't appear. The judge winces and warns that if arresting officers don't show, he's going to start dismissing cases.

That's when I realize that the judge is standing and wincing because he has hemorrhoids.

My docket is called. The arresting officer isn't in court. The judge says, "This is the third scheduled pretrial hearing today where the arresting officer hasn't shown up. This case is dismissed."

I've never felt greater relief.

I thank the judge and leave the courthouse with my father and lawyer, grateful that the judge has hemorrhoids.

1968

Resist the draft

I continue to take graduate classes at C.W.Post College as the Vietnam War rages on with horrific suffering on all sides. Our country is torn apart by hostilities between people who support the war and people who oppose it. Clashes between pro and anti-war demonstrators escalate as the cruelties of war play out on the nightly news.

I experience this deep divide firsthand while driving in my Volkswagen bug to a house I share with two college students in Greenvale, New York, on Long Island.

On the rear bumper of my car is a sticker that reads: "RESIST THE DRAFT." I drive down an off-ramp on Long Island and pause at a stop sign. A car pulls up behind me and the driver honks his horn. I look in my rearview mirror and see a man shake a fist at me. He accelerates his car and smashes into my rear bumper. Then he backs up and stops. Through my rearview mirror, I see him shake a fist at me again.

I shift into reverse and accelerate into the front of his car. I drive back to the stop sign and wave to him. He slams into my car again. I slam into his. We do this three times and then I drive away. My car repair is expensive.

1968

The dog burning

A few weeks after getting my car repaired, I come up with an idea for an anti-war protest that might cause people who support the war in Vietnam to rethink their position and join the anti-war movement.

I phone a local Long Island newspaper and give a made-up name for myself to someone in the news department. I say that I'm the leader of Students Against the War, and at noon on November 7, at the C.W.Post campus flagpole, we're going to burn a dog with napalm to show the effects of napalm being used by the U.S. in Vietnam against the Vietnamese people.

The newspaper prints the information I've given and days later, they print letters from outraged readers. One letter mentions that the local ASPCA has received phone calls telling them not to give a dog to any hippies.

I set up a table in the C.W.Post College cafeteria with a sign that reads: "Please sign a petition to protest the burning of a dog with napalm on November 7th at the campus flagpole." In one week, I gather more than two hundred signatures on the petition from angry students. Using a different alias and wearing a hat, I drop off the petition at the local newspaper, which prints the information.

Wearing a back pack, I take a train to New York City and go to the War Resisters League. I tell them I'm planning an anti-war protest on Long Island and I need a lot of pamphlets to hand out. They tell me to take as many as I want, they'll get more. I take three hundred, place them in my back pack and return to the house I share in Greenvale, New York.

I tell my roommates, Aaron and Dave, about the anti-war protest I'm planning for November 7th and ask if they'll help me with it. They say yes.

The following week, in the living room of our house, we pair three hundred War Resisters League pamphlets with three hundred xeroxed and folded sheets of paper that I printed, which, when opened, read: "Thank you for saving an innocent dog from being burned with napalm. Now please turn your attention and protest to the war in Vietnam where American planes are dropping napalm on Vietnamese people. Help end the Vietnam war!"

We make three large signs that each read: "STOP THE DOG BURNING! JOIN US AT THE FLAGPOLE TODAY AT NOON!"

On November 7th, at 11:30 a.m., carrying the signs we've made, Aaron, Dave and I lead a march of nine students that grows to twenty by the time we get to the flagpole at 11:45. We join a large crowd that has gathered there, waiting for the dog burners to arrive with a dog.

The three of us leave the crowd and go to our cars in a nearby student parking lot. We each lift from our car's trunk a box containing one hundred pamphlets and one hundred folded sheets of paper. I also take a bullhorn that I've rented. I carry the box and bullhorn to the outer edge of the crowd near the flagpole, joining Aaron and Dave, who are there with their boxes.

Naomi approaches us and I introduce her to my roommates. She's an activist, known for giving great speeches at anti-war rallies in Nassau County. I had called her and talked about the anti-war protest I was planning. She liked the concept. I asked if she would give a speech and she said yes.

She asks, “Are we ready to start?”

“We’re ready,” I say, handing her the bullhorn. She walks through the crowd of several hundred students who are waiting to confront the dog burner. I scan the crowd and see two men dressed for professional work. FBI? Undercover police?

Naomi stops at an open space in front of the flagpole. She turns around and launches into an impassioned anti-war speech, as Aaron, Dave and I hand out pamphlets and folded paper to everyone who has gathered there.

Surprise, reflection and annoyance ripple through the crowd as they read: “Thank you for saving an innocent dog from being burned with napalm. Now please turn your attention and protest to the war in Vietnam where American planes are dropping napalm on Vietnamese people. Help end the Vietnam war!”

Someone yells “Where’s the dog? You were gonna burn a dog with napalm!”

Another shouts, “Yeah! Where’s the dog?”

Naomi ignores them and finishes her speech, to light applause. The crowd turns eerily quiet.

I thank Aaron and Dave and tell them I’ll see them later. Naomi hands me the bullhorn.

“Great speech,” I say as we walk toward her car in the parking lot.

We’re being followed. I turn around and see the two men from the dog burning protest, the ones I thought might be undercover police. They’re definitely not students.

Naomi turns around. The men stop walking. “Undercover cops,” she says.

We walk to her car, I thank her, and she drives away. As I head to my car, I look for the two men who were following us. They’re gone. I drive home, wondering if I’ve crossed over a line I couldn’t see.

A few weeks later, I’m walking on the C.W.Post campus after a class. A man walks toward me. He looks five or six years older than most of the students at the College. I've seen him before at two of our on-campus anti-war protests. He has black hair and a black goatee. So do I.

He stops near me and says, "Hi. Do you have a minute to talk?"

"Who's asking?"

"Terry. I'm a student here. I've been to two anti-war protests at the College. I was at the last one – the dog burning. That was a mind blower."

"It was meant to be. Yeah, I remember seeing you."

"Was the dog burning your idea?"

"What difference does that make?"

"None. Just asking."

"Why did you stop me?"

"Can I trust you?"

"To do what?"

"To keep a small bomb for two weeks while I'm away?"

"Are you out of your mind? I'm a non-violent person."

"No harm in asking."

I tell him, "We're trying to stop violence, not create more." I continue on my way.

At our house in Greenvale, I tell Aaron and Dave what happened on campus with a guy named Terry asking me to store a bomb for two weeks. I give a description of him and say, "I think he's an undercover cop. Spread the word." They say they will.

December, 1968

I see white knuckles

I complete my graduate courses at C.W.Post College and I'm able to keep my draft deferment by being hired to teach English at Francis Lewis High School in Fresh Meadows, New York. My first day teaching, I walk into a classroom with about twenty-five tenth graders sitting at desks. Four are seated in the last row, laughing as I enter the room. I introduce myself and begin my class. They keep laughing. I ask them what's so funny? Several students point to a window, which I walk to and look outside. I see white knuckles on two hands holding on to the ledge, two stories above the pavement. I open the window and pull in the student who had been placed there to hang with the window closed. Besides being traumatized for life, the student is OK.

I continue to live with my two roommates in Greenvale, Long Island, and I commute to Francis Lewis High School to teach.

The beginning of May, 1969

Something's coming

After returning from teaching at Francis Lewis High School, Dave tells Aaron and me, "I was standing on the front porch this morning and a cop in uniform walks past on the sidewalk. He looks at me for maybe two seconds as he passes, before continuing on his way."

We've never seen a policeman walk past the house before. I think about the dog burning protest and wonder if they're coming for me because I violated some protest ordinance. Or maybe they're coming for Dave because he buys a small amount of marijuana every few months. I'm worried.

Early evening, the following day, when I walk upstairs to my room, I don't turn on the light. I walk to my bedroom window, part the curtain a few inches and look outside. I see a police car parked facing the street in a driveway across from our house. The car is visible in the light from a street lamp. I close the curtain and feel sure now that someone in the house is about to be busted.

I go downstairs and tell Dave and Aaron what I saw. Aaron turns off the lights in the living room and pulls back the curtain, just enough so he can look out the window. "The cop car's gone," he says.

I'm on high alert. "Something's about to happen," I tell them. "Dave, maybe you should hide your stash better."

He laughs. "They're not going to look in the freezer behind a few frozen steaks and vegetables."

"Probably not," I say. I go upstairs to my room and get in bed, but I don't fall asleep for several hours.

At six in the morning, Dave knocks on my bedroom door. He tells me there are two men at the front door who want to speak with me. I go downstairs wearing pajamas and a robe. I open the front door and two men in plain clothes flash badges. One has a moustache. The other is stout.

The one with the moustache asks, "Are you Charles Scott Seldin?" I say yes. He says, "You're under arrest for sale and possession of a dangerous drug. Get dressed. We're taking you in."

I'm shocked and confused by the charge. I've occasionally smoked marijuana, but I never sold any drug to anyone.

The stout man asks, "OK if we look around your house?"

Dave says, "Do you have a search warrant?"

"No."

"Then you can't look around."

The stout man tells me, "Get dressed." As he follows me up the stairs to my room, I wonder if there will be a newspaper photographer or a TV news crew at the courthouse when I'm taken there. In case that happens, I decide to wear a suit and tie.

The stout man stands at the entrance to my room and watches as I take my only suit and tie from the closet and place them on my bed.

Annoyed, he says, "Just put on some clothes. You're not going to a wedding."

"I feel like wearing a suit and tie."

Handcuffed, wearing my suit and tie, I'm driven to a police precinct to be booked, photographed and fingerprinted. Then I'm taken to the Nassau County Courthouse. As I get out of the car, I see several handcuffed college-age men and women led by policemen past a local TV crew filming them as they enter the courthouse. I know one of them. He's an anti-war activist and I can't imagine him selling drugs, if that's what he's been arrested for.

As I enter the courtroom, the trauma of what's happening hits hard.

In the large room, I sit alone on a long bench. Thirty or forty people sit on benches throughout the room, waiting to be called before a judge who presides in front of us. I look around the room and see two more students I know who helped organize anti-war protests at C.W.Post College.

I would later learn that more than fifty people had been arrested in what was described as Nassau County's largest drug bust. I would also later learn that the mass arrest was front page news in the *New York Times*, with the names of everyone arrested published, including mine.

A well-dressed man sitting behind me leans forward and says, "It's terrible what they're doing to these kids."

I turn around and look at him. I ask, "Are you a lawyer?"

"Yes," he says. "My name is Ernest Peace."

That's all I need to hear. His name is Ernest Peace. "Mr. Peace," I say, "I'm innocent. I've never sold a drug to anyone in my life." I don't expect him to believe me just because I say it, but I have to say it anyway. "I'm being framed. Will you represent me before the judge today?"

He says yes and hands me his business card. I ask him to call my parents and tell them I've been arrested and why. He takes a pad and pen from his briefcase and writes the information I give him. I add, "I'm a teacher at Francis Lewis High School in Fresh Meadows, New York. Please ask my father to call there and let them know what's happened." He says he will and he jots down the name of the school.

I'm called before the judge. Mr. Peace stands next to me. I plead not guilty to sale and possession of an illegal drug, marijuana.

I'm led to a police car and driven to the Nassau County Jail where I'm photographed, my hair is cut short, and my goatee is shaved off. I'm photographed again, led to a shower, told to take off my clothes and handed a bar of soap. I shower, dry myself with a towel and put my clothes back on. Emotionally, I'm reeling and outraged.

Allowed one phone call, I call Sandy, a woman I'd met a month before at a Yale drama festival in Connecticut. I tell her what's happened and ask if she'll visit me at the Nassau County jail. She says she'll see me the following day.

A guard walks me to a cell on a block of cells and locks me in. I sit on the end of the cell's bed and it's clear to me why I've been arrested on trumped-up drug charges. To the powers that be in Nassau County, my anti-war "dog burning" protest, while legal, crossed the line between acceptable and unacceptable protest. I've been shut down. After I'm out on bail, I'll have to be careful to not get arrested again at an anti-war demonstration.

Rock music plays so loud on the cell block that I struggle to hear myself think. I'm falling apart.

A guard passes by. I call to him. He stops and steps up to my cell's bars. "Guard," I say, "I'm having a very rough time. I'm innocent. I need to talk with someone."

He says, "I'll see what I can do." He returns a few hours later and takes me to see Dr. Williams, the jail's psychologist. Outside Dr. Williams' office, the guard says, "I'll wait for you here."

In his office, Dr. Williams sits behind a desk. I sit on a chair facing him. He asks, "Why have you asked to see me?" His face is expressionless.

"I'm being framed on a drug charge. I'm innocent."

"You'll have your day in court," he says.

"I need your help right now," I reply. "I'm locked in a cell, isolated, claustrophobic. The only people I see are guards walking by."

He's unmoved. "There's nothing I can do about your situation."

"You *can* do something," I tell him. "I need to see and talk with other people. You can recommend that for my mental health they unlock my cell door and let me talk with everyone on my cell block."

"That wouldn't be fair to people who would remain locked in their cells."

"I would talk with all of them," I say. "They're feeling as isolated and alone as I am. They would benefit and I would also."

"Sorry. I can't do that."

"Dr. Williams," I say, "I'm starting to lose it. I know you can ask the right person to let me out of my cell during the day. I'm not asking for much. I'm not trying to escape."

"It's not going to happen," he says.

My rage and despair intensify. Dr. Williams," I say, "I'm an innocent man in a jail cell facing serious charges. I'm accused of something I didn't do. If I don't get to see other people, I'm going to have a breakdown and if that happens, when they take me out of my cell, there will be one name I'll be calling out, and it will be your name, Dr. Williams, because you can help me right now, and no one else can."

"I wish I could help, but I can't," he says. "You can go now."

The guard outside his office returns me to my cell.

Later that afternoon, a guard opens my cell door and tells me I'm free to talk with anyone on the cell block until eight at night when I'll be locked in again.

I talk with people up and down the cell block. They tell me why they're here. I tell them what happened to me. We connect. Many are students. Some are drug dealers. Some are student activists who tell me they're being framed with drug charges. They say they're innocent. I tell them I am also.

I'm starting to get the big picture. They've busted a lot of drug dealers and mixed in people who create protests against the war in Vietnam.

The next day, a guard drops off clean underwear and socks. "From your parents," he says. That afternoon, Sandy visits me. Separated by a glass partition, talking through phones, our bond is powerful. Her visit helps stabilize me.

I'm released from jail on Monday morning. My parents pick me up and I follow their car in mine to their house in Croton. There, I tell them what happened and that I'm innocent. They believe me with unconditional love. A few weeks later, I phone Mr. Peace and learn that I'm accused of selling a half ounce of marijuana.

I begin to piece my life back together. I know it's going to take time. Maybe a lifetime.

Eleven months after being arrested — eleven months after my friends disappeared because I was considered too hot to be around – eleven months during which time I married Sandy, worked in my father's small mail order business and lived in Little Italy, Manhattan – I receive notice that jury selection will begin on April 14,1970, if my case goes to trial.

April 14, 1970, I meet my father and my lawyer, Mr. Peace, in the Nassau County Courthouse. We sit on a bench in the large room, which is half-filled with people waiting with lawyers.

Mr. Peace tells me and my father that he's going to meet with the

Nassau County prosecutor in a conference room to discuss my case. I tell him again that I'm innocent and I'm not going to plead guilty to anything I didn't do.

He leaves the courthouse. I sit with my father and we listen as a presiding judge hears cases.

When Mr. Peace returns from his meeting, he tells us that the prosecutor is willing to reduce the felony charges against me to a misdemeanor, if I agree to plead guilty. I refuse the offer.

He advises, "This is Nassau County, which is very Republican. If we go to trial, know that the prosecutor has never lost a drug case."

"I understand what I'm up against," I say.

"One other thing," he adds. "An undercover witness for the prosecution in your case was in the conference room with the assistant district attorney and me. They say they've got a solid case against you."

"What does the undercover witness look like?" I ask.

"Medium height, about twenty-five, black hair, black goatee."

My jaw drops. "That's the guy who asked me to store a bomb for two weeks."

"Still," Mr. Peace says, "it will be your word against his. Are you sure you don't want to plead guilty to a misdemeanor and not go to trial?"

"I'm sure. I'll get statements from the people I told about the man who asked me to store a bomb for two weeks."

"OK," Mr. Peace says. "It's your decision." He leaves the courthouse to meet again with the assistant district attorney. When he returns, a half hour later, he tells us that the prosecutor has offered to reduce the charges to disorderly conduct, if I plead guilty, and if I say no, he's ready to go to trial."

"Disorderly conduct?" I say, incredulous. "I've been framed on a phony drug charge, waiting for eleven months to go to trial and they want me to plead guilty to disorderly conduct? Reduced from sale and possession of marijuana? I'll accept the charge of disorderly conduct, while maintaining my innocence."

He looks doubtful. "I don't know if they'll accept that."

I'm disgusted. "If they can reduce a felony charge for sale and possession of marijuana to disorderly conduct, then they have no case against me and they know it."

Mr. Peace says nothing in response. He returns to the conference room.

An hour later, I'm standing in front of judge David T. Gibbons. My lawyer stands about five feet to my right. The assistant district attorney stands about ten feet to my left.

Here is the complete sixteen-page transcript as it appears in the copy I have. Please note that my name in the transcript is spelled Charles Scott Seldon. It should be Charles Scott Seldin.

COUNTY COURT
Nassau County
THE PEOPLE OF THE STATE OF NEW YORK
-against-
CHARLES SCOTT SELDON, Ind. #1789 Defendant. \
Mineola, New York

April 14, 1970

Before: HON. DAVID T. GIBBONS, County Court Judge.

Appearances: BARRY BRENAN, ESQ. for the People.

Assistant District Attorney ERNEST PEACE, ESQ. for the defendant.

MINUTES OF CHANGE OF PLEA AND SENTENCE

MICHAEL YESNER Official Court Reporter

THE COURT: All right. Before I accept the plea I will ask the defendant some questions. You are Scott Seldon?

THE DEFENDANT: Yes, I am.

THE COURT: How old are you?"

THE DEFENDANT: I am 25

THE COURT: Excuse me?

THE DEFENDANT: 25.
THE COURT: Are you married?

THE DEFENDANT: Yes, I am.

THE COURT: Were any promises made to you with respect to punishment or sentence by the Court, the District Attorney, your attorney or anybody?

THE DEFENDANT: No.

THE COURT: Did anybody force you into taking this plea or are you doing it of your own free will?

THE DEFENDANT: On my own.

THE COURT: And have you talked this over with your attorney?

THE DEFENDANT: Yes

THE COURT: And with your family?
THE DEFENDANT: Yes

THE COURT: And your family is here in the court?

THE DEFENDANT: My father is in court.

THE COURT: Do you know that when you plead guilty to a violation, disorderly conduct, which is a violation, I can send you to jail for up to fifteen days or I can give you a conditional discharge under which conditions I can impose certain sanctions and requirements on you?

THE DEFENDANT: I understand that.

THE COURT: Now, you know that when you plead guilty to this you are not pleading guilty to a crime but, nevertheless, some place, somewhere, sometime it's going to show up on the record that you have been convicted of disorderly conduct: do you understand that?

THE DEFENDANT: Yes

THE COURT: And, particularly, it's going to refer to, if I understand this correctly, it's going to refer to subdivision 7, which says, "A person is guilty of disorderly conduct when with intent to cause public inconvenience, annoyance or alarm, or recklessly creating a risk thereof, he creates a hazardous or physically offensive condition by any act which serves no legitimate purpose." That's what will be on your record: do you understand that?

THE DEFENDANT: I understand that.

THE COURT: At present are you under the influence of any drugs or intoxicants?

THE DEFENDANT: No, I am not.

THE COURT: Are you suffering from any physical or mental disability which would in any way prevent you from pleading here today?
THE DEFENDANT: The only mental anguish is pleading guilty to something I didn't do. Other than that, I have no condition which would prevent me from taking this plea.

THE COURT: Now, I just want to tell you, Mr. Seldon, that I have before me an indictment, No. 27189, and with respect to that indictment you are charged with several counts of criminally selling a dangerous drug and criminally possessing a dangerous drug. If you want, you have the right to go to trial with respect to these charges set forth in the indictment, and in going to trial there would be in your favor a presumption of innocence.

The People would have the burden of proof throughout the case, and up until the time and even during the period of deliberation they would have to prove your guilt beyond a reasonable doubt. You would have the right to confront your accusers. The People would present witnesses and you could cross-examine them. Your attorney, of course, would do that on your behalf. You could present witnesses in your own behalf. Alibi witnesses as well as any other type of witnesses that you wish to present, character witness and so forth. So you would be entitled to a full-scale jury trial with all of the constitutional protections afforded to you by the Code of Criminal procedure and the laws of the State of New York and the United States.

All of these you have going for you if you wish to go to trial. If you plead you are just not going to have a trial: do you understand that?

THE DEFENDANT: I understand that.

THE COURT: Do you want to give up your right to a jury trial and plead guilty to disorderly conduct?

THE DEFENDANT: I wish to do that.

THE COURT: Now, I just want to say one other thing: It's not usual for me to accept a plea from a man who says that he is not guilty. I am aware of People against Serrano, 15 New York 2d, which says that even though a man is not guilty, if he wants to plead – or, I should say, even if a man asserts that he is not guilty, and he wants to plead on the very serious charges set forth in the indictment where the risk of punishment would be great, the court can accept his plea. I am not much on doing that, very frankly. I feel most reluctant to accept a plea from a man who says that he is not guilty.

Now, let me just ask you about this: Is it your contention, then, Mr. Seldon, that you did not at any time sell a dangerous drug, or possess any dangerous drug, and I am referring specifically now to on or about the 6th day of February, 1969: is that your contention?

THE DEFENDANT: I have never sold or in any way accommodated

any drug whatsoever.

THE COURT: And you haven't possessed any?

THE DEFENDANT: I have had no relationship with drugs.

THE COURT: And it's your contention that you never have?

THE DEFENDANT: I have had no relationship whatever with drugs.

THE COURT: Well, you can understand, then, Mr. Seldon, my reluctance to accept this plea unless you can give me some good reason why I should. Why do you want me to take your plea to disorderly conduct when it's your contention that you have never committed any crime? You know, I am here for the purpose of upholding justice, and I want in no way to subvert justice. Why do you feel that it would be just for me to accept your plea?

THE DEFENDANT: This is a very complicated situation, and it's taken a great deal of thought on my part to come to this conclusion. It's very difficult to accept a guilty plea when you know that there is no truth whatsoever to the charge. It's very difficult to accept this plea when you have subjected yourself and your family and the people you know to such a difficult situation, put them under such stress, but I feel that when I look at the situation and I look at the years of schooling that I have had, going to graduate school to become a teacher, and the fact that I was teaching before the arrest, that my license was taken from me after this arrest, and that a felony conviction would end my teaching career as well as end possibilities for other jobs, I feel that, weighing all of these things, it is the most pragmatic approach to take a guilty plea to a disorderly conduct charge which would permit me to teach and permit me to pursue what my education has allowed me the possibility of pursuing.

THE COURT: Well, how about the fact that you then will have a disorderly conduct on your record and the possibility that someone may say, "Well, look, you must have done something because you pled guilty to disorderly conduct, and if you weren't guilty, you wouldn't have pled." Supposing you are faced with that situation? Will that in any way hamper your progress in your chosen career?

DEFENDANT: It may do so, but I feel that I have enough faith in human beings so that in a situation where somebody might look at a disorderly conduct charge and say, "What is this about?", I have enough faith in that human being to believe that I could explain this situation to that person and have him believe me, and I feel that with this faith I can accept this plea.

THE COURT: Well, let me say this: This is the position of the Court: The Court is most reluctant to accept a plea, except that you are, you might say, attempting to persuade the Court to accept it on the basis of your desire not to run the risk of the serious penalties that could be imposed if you were found guilty and the problem that it would create with respect to your career: is that the essence of what's involved here? You contend that you are not guilty?

THE DEFENDANT: Yes.

THE COURT: And, yet, you want to plead to something because you don't want to run the risk of a conviction where the penalty for the crime might not only be harsh but in addition you would be faced with this to haunt you in the future, a conviction for a felony: is that about the essence of it?

THE DEFENDANT: That's the essence of the situation.
MR. PEACE: May I make a comment for the record, your Honor?

THE COURT: Yes.

MR. PEACE: In our discussion prior to the acceptance of this plea I informed Mr. Seldon that he would get, certainly, a fair trial in this court, that the District Attorney would treat him fairly, that in this case, as he believes, I believe that the policeman has made a mistake. However, I also advised him that probably we would prevail at trial but there would be no way that I could guarantee an acquittal in this trial, no matter what evidence we presented, and it was on this basis then, that he and I felt – and I do agree with his taking this plea — that a plea to disorderly conduct would permit him to continue in his chosen profession and that the odds on his acquittal are not commensurate with the terrible price he would pay in the event of a conviction.

THE COURT: All right. I won't even ask him anything about the underlying facts concerning the alleged crime because as far as I am concerned the sole purpose of his taking this plea, from what he has stated to me, and I can accept it on no other basis, is that he wants to avoid going to trial on the very serious charges set forth in the indictment where if he were convicted the punishment or penalty might be greater and he would then be faced with this stigma as an impediment to his career from there on.

All right, the Court will accept the plea, reluctantly, I might say, and it is the first time that I know of that I have accepted a plea under these conditions and I do it most reluctantly.

THE CLERK: Charles Scott Seldon, you wish to withdraw your plea of not guilty heretofore entered and at this time plead guilty to disorderly conduct in full satisfaction of this indictment?

THE DEFENDANT: I do.

THE CLERK: How do you plead, guilty or not guilty?

THE DEFENDANT: I plead guilty to the disorderly conduct charge.

THE CLERK: Your Honor, the defendant pleads guilty. Date of sentence?

MR PEACE: First, I will waive all motions that may be pending before the Court in this matter and waive any statutory right to a delay and request that the Court sentence the defendant at this time.

THE COURT: All right.

THE CLERK: You are entitled to a legal delay of 48 hours before judgment is pronounced against you. Do you wish to waive that delay and be sentenced now?

THE DEFENDANT: I do.

THE CLERK: Have you any legal cause to show why judgment should not be pronounced against you?

THE DEFENDANT: No.

THE CLERK: Give your attention to Judge Gibbons.

THE COURT: I will pronounce sentence at this time, and I just want to say that everything I have done here today is somewhat not in keeping with my general approach to people who come before the bar of justice.

I must consider the fact that this man's future is at stake. I must also consider the fact that the District Attorney must have had a weak case and perhaps even a case that was practically nonexistent when he will offer a plea of disorderly conduct. I accepted the man's plea to disorderly conduct after he told me that he was not guilty of any crime at all, and I did it on the basis that was stated on the record, that the young man wants to save his future and can't run the risk of the possibility that a jury might believe what evidence is presented against him.

I am going to continue as a sentence to keep in mind the manner in which this was presented to me, that is, the District Attorney's offer of a plea of disorderly conduct, which must indicate that there is little or no case on the part of the People, and the defendant says that he is not guilty of any crime at all, and his attorney gives me his assurance in conference in chambers as well as here that it is his firm opinion that this young man is not guilty of anything at all. So we have done what I am most reluctant to do. I have accepted a plea from a man who claims that he is not guilty and there is nothing which appears to contradict that from the very manner in which the case was presented to me.

So, under the circumstances, having done this and now being faced with the distasteful task of imposing sentence, the best thing I can do, and I will do, is to relieve this man, then, from any other inconvenience that may be afforded through this Court, and I, therefore, sentence you on your plea of guilty to disorderly conduct to unconditional discharge.

That is the judgment of the Court.

MR. PEACE: Thank you very much, your Honor.

MR. BRENNAN: Your Honor, with your permission, in view of your remarks, I would like to place at least something on the record. Had there been little or no case I would have moved to dismiss. My motivation in offering this plea had to do with the preservation of the cover of the two undercover agents of the police department and a civilian unknown Informant – known to me – and that had something to do with my motivation. Had there been no case, your Honor, I would like the record to be clear that I would have dismissed it.

THE COURT: Well, I will have to remark, and I don't want to engage in controversy, that I only want to say any time an undercover man makes an arrest – and in this case it wasn't even an arrest, I am assuming, because there would be no question if there were an arrest— I could only say that the undercover man has to be exposed. So the very fact that an indictment has been brought indicates that the undercover man is going to be exposed. So why in a case like this do we say that we are giving a disorderly conduct to preserve the anonymity of the undercover man?

All right: that's the judgment of the Court.

MR. PEACE: Thank you very much, your Honor.

CERTIFICATION: I hereby certify this is an accurate transcript.
(signed by) Michael Yesner Official Court Reporter

I walk out of the courtroom with my father and Mr. Peace, who says to me, "You must feel a lot better now than you did when you came here this morning."

"Yes," I say, "but I'm also angry about being framed and losing my teaching job and the terrible toll this has taken on me, my family and people I'm close to."

I thank Mr. Peace for representing me. I shake hands with him and he leaves the courtroom.

My father and I hug, relieved. I thank him and tell him how grateful I am for his support and the support that others have shown me. We stop at a pay phone. I call my mother and Sandy and tell them what happened in court. My father drives back to Croton after dropping me off at a train station. I return to New York City and begin the long process of recovering from this nightmare.

1971

To kill and be killed

I'm no longer awaiting trial and I'm not in graduate school and I'm not teaching high school. On February 5, 1971, I'm called before my draft board and a few weeks later my selective service classification is changed from I-Y to 1-A. I can be inducted into the army at any time before my birthday on March 15, when I'll turn twenty-six and will no longer be eligible for the draft.

I talk with a lawyer who specializes in draft cases. He suggests that I write a letter to my draft board in a circular way about my recent meeting with them, including references to errors they may have made that could be challenged legally. He suggests a few possibilities.

I write the following to my draft board.

Local Board #12
7 Bank Street
Peekskill, New York 10566

Gentlemen,

On January 12, 1971, you were kind enough to give me the opportunity to appear before you personally and on January 13, 1971, you mailed me a notification that despite my past efforts to convince you to the contrary you had maintained me in a 1-A classification. What happened was sort of like this, generally speaking, and I have to speak generally because you would not let me have a tape recorder anyway, or a stenographer and you would not let me hire and bring with me my lawyer who would have been able to explain to me what was going on, even though I tried to find out by asking questions and a lawyer would have been able to do it better but, what happened was that you asked me why I thought I was entitled to a different classification and I said that there were lots of reasons including the fact that I was politically opposed to the whole idea of a military apparatus in general and war altogether but most of all was made physically and morally sick by the outrageous actions of this country in Vietnam. I said that I was mentally out of tune with the whole war including the song they were playing in Vietnam and they asked me why I hadn't applied for conscientious objection and I said that I might even be qualified for one and that I had been thinking about it for a long time, years as a matter of fact, but there were a few minor points I had to work out before I could decide whether I was qualified and that I would let them know when I had them worked out. One of the members asked me whether I would accept a 1-AO classification and I said that I would not because that would only be patching men up to send them back to war to kill and be killed and besides it was like being part of the whole bad song in Vietnam anyway and the Board member then told me that the kind of men they would send me to patch up would be so badly injured that they could not be sent back to battle and I told them I did not know how he could know that and, besides, it would be part of the whole thing anyway and that I would not do it. I pointed out that I had been classified 1-Y because I was morally unfit to be a member of the Army, but the Board members told me that I-Y was only for physical things but I told them to look at my file which would prove to them that they were wrong and I told them that I was at least as morally unfit now as I had been officially recognized as morally unfit and I asked how they could have changed my classification when my morality had not gotten any better. They asked me about my second arrest and I explained I had copped a plea to disorderly conduct to settle a charge of sale and possession of marijuana and the Board members thought that was pretty funny and one of them couldn't understand how it could happen and another Board member explained to him that it must be because I had a pretty smart lawyer and this made me mad and I said so and I explained that the reason the charges were reduced was that this is the way the criminal law works in this country where they charge you with more than they can prove in order to blackmail you into taking a plea to something you did not do anyway and one of the Board members asked whether I did not have any faith in the American judicial system and I told them that I did not and I was amazed that they still did. But the subject changed and they asked me when my birthday was and they told me that they could still draft me after I was 26 and I appeal the result now but I told them then that I am sure they cannot and they had a long discussion among themselves whether they could or couldn't and the secretary said that she didn't know and one of them said that he thought they could not but another member was just as clear and definite in saying that they could and I know that they can't but it doesn't really matter because I am just as entitled to the moral disqualification now as I was in the first place and I am clearly a personality type which can clearly not get along in the military and I said so and they asked me whether they should send me for a physical and I told them that it was up to them and then one of them asked me what I was doing for my country and I told him that I was acting in the way that I thought was best serving the interests of the people of the country but that was not the same thing as serving the government which happened to be in power.

At this point, they said that they would let me know and I left. I believe everything I have said is accurate and complete and I ask that I be advised in writing of anything which I have said that is not accurate or of anything which I have left out.

Charles Scott Seldin
59 Thompson Street

New York, New York 10012

I never hear from the draft board again. I turn twenty-six and the tragic wake of the Vietnam war subdues any feeling of celebration.

1972

Spirit stirs

Sandy and I are living in a cottage we've rented in Shady, New York, a ten-minute drive to the nearby town of Woodstock. We seek the peace and space of country life and an unwinding from New York City and the turmoil of the Vietnam war. With that in mind, we join a small group that meditates once a week in Woodstock.

I begin reading books about the lives of spiritual masters, beginning with *Autobiography of a Yogi* by Paramhansa Yogananda. In his book, Yogananda describes his journey to Self-realization, guided by his guru, Sri Yuktaswar. As I meditate and read, I'm awakened to myself as a spiritual being.

In words that ring true, Yogananda shares his experience in cosmic consciousness and his recollections of previous incarnations – "glimpses of the past, by some dimensionless link…."[3]

The ancient spiritual teachings revealed in Yogananda's book give me a context for the glimpses of a dimensionless link that I experienced when I rescued my brother, Clem, from the top of a boulder where he had climbed to escape snakes and when I saw the spirit form of my cousin Michael, the night that he died.

1972

Bob Dylan slept here

Bob Dylan lives in Woodstock, New York. One of Sandy's friends is friends with the caretaker of Dylan's house while he and his family are away for a few weeks. Sandy's friend tells her that Dylan told the caretaker that he could invite a few friends over for short periods of time.

Sandy's friend talks with the caretaker and arranges a time for us to stop by Dylan's house for a brief visit.

On a crisp, golden fall day, I drive Sandy in my car up a long unpaved road leading to a large, wood country home. We enter the living room and smell ashes before we see the floor-to-ceiling stone fireplace with several burned logs in it. The stones directly above the fireplace opening have a carbon-colored cast to them.

A large black and white photograph of Dylan hangs halfway up the tall fireplace chimney. He is in a recording studio, seated at a piano, playing a harmonica which hangs around his neck.

About a year and a half later, Dylan releases his album *Planet Waves* and sings

"On a night like this," with these lyrics:

"Build a fire throw on logs
And listen to it hiss
And let it burn, burn, burn, burn
On a night like this"[4]

Feeling a little uncomfortable with who I'm turning out to be at this moment, I walk to his stereo and record collection and thumb through his records. By now, I'm really disgusted with myself.

The only Bob Dylan album he has is "Nashville Skyline," which was released in 1969. He has many folk records, including several Woody Guthrie and Joan Baez albums. And several Frank Sinatra albums. This surprises me. Frank Sinatra was a great singer, but Frank Sinatra? Then I realize that Sinatra and Dylan both phrase lyrics in original, expressive ways.

I walk upstairs into a bedroom and there it is – a big brass bed. Dylan's song, "Lay lady lay," plays in my head:

"Lay lady lay
Lay across my big brass bed
Whatever colors you have in your mind

I'll show them to you and you'll see them shine."[5]

About five feet in front of the bed, leaning against a wall, is a six-foot-long abstract painting, signed by Jann Wenner, founder and publisher of *Rolling Stone* magazine.

I ask myself: Would you want a stranger looking at your bed in your bedroom? I leave the room and walk downstairs to the living room. Sandy and the caretaker are sitting in comfortable chairs talking to each other. I enter a study that has a desk and a large bookcase filled with books, many of which were in my parents' house and the houses of many of their progressive friends in Croton-on-Hudson – authors like John Steinbeck, Ernest Hemingway, Dos Pasos, Thomas Wolfe, Jack London, Hermann Hesse, Tennessee Williams, as well as many of the beat generation: Allan Ginsberg, William Burroughs, Paul Bowles, Jack Kerouac, Lawrence Ferlinghetti.

I leave his study and peer into a large room off the living room, filled with children's toys, including a large rocking horse.

We only stay fifteen or twenty minutes. Thank you, Bob Dylan, for all that you've given me, and forgive me for being like everyone else whose life has been so deeply affected by your songs.

Spring, 1974

Out of the blue

Sandy and I are living in San Miguel de Allende, Mexico. We're both enrolled in Master of Fine Arts programs at The Instituto Allende, which is part of the University of Guanajuato — painting for Sandy, creative writing for me.

Before spring semester begins, we drive with Sandy's friend, Diane, toward the west coast of Mexico. It's a Sunday and I drive my '66 Buick through the sparsely populated countryside, past a few cattle grazing in fields, with no towns or people seen for many miles.

Without warning, smoke rises from my car's hood, followed by a loss of power. The car coasts to a stop at a rest area where two men sit at a picnic table near a pickup truck. I get out of my car and lift the hood. The battery cables are smoldering. I curse and curse some more. The two men approach me, smiling and laughing, talking to each other. I think they're Mexican, but I'm not sure. They look under the hood at the battery cables and one of the men speaks to me. I don't understand what he says. I tell him, "Habla un poco."

Sandy and Diane join us. One of the men walks to the pickup truck, reaches over the low sidewalls into the bed and lifts out two battery cables and a pair of pliers. He returns to my car, where he loosens and removes the burned cables and begins to replace them with new ones. I walk to his truck and look over the sidewalls. There's nothing else in the bed.

I return to my car as the man tightens the new cables in place. He looks at me and smiles. I motion with my arms toward the sky and say, "It's as if you came from above." The men laugh. I take money from my wallet but it's waved away.

"Gracias! Gracias," I say. The men walk to the pickup truck and drive away. We get in my car and continue our trip to the west coast of Mexico.

Summer, 1974

A world in grains of sand

Before fall semester begins at The Instituto Allende, I'm walking with my camera on a west coast beach in Mexico when I come upon sand with minerals visible in it. The minerals create abstract images which, to me, are free-form expressions of Spirit.

I photograph them and make prints for a photography class that I'm taking at The Instituto Allende. Here are three of these photographs.

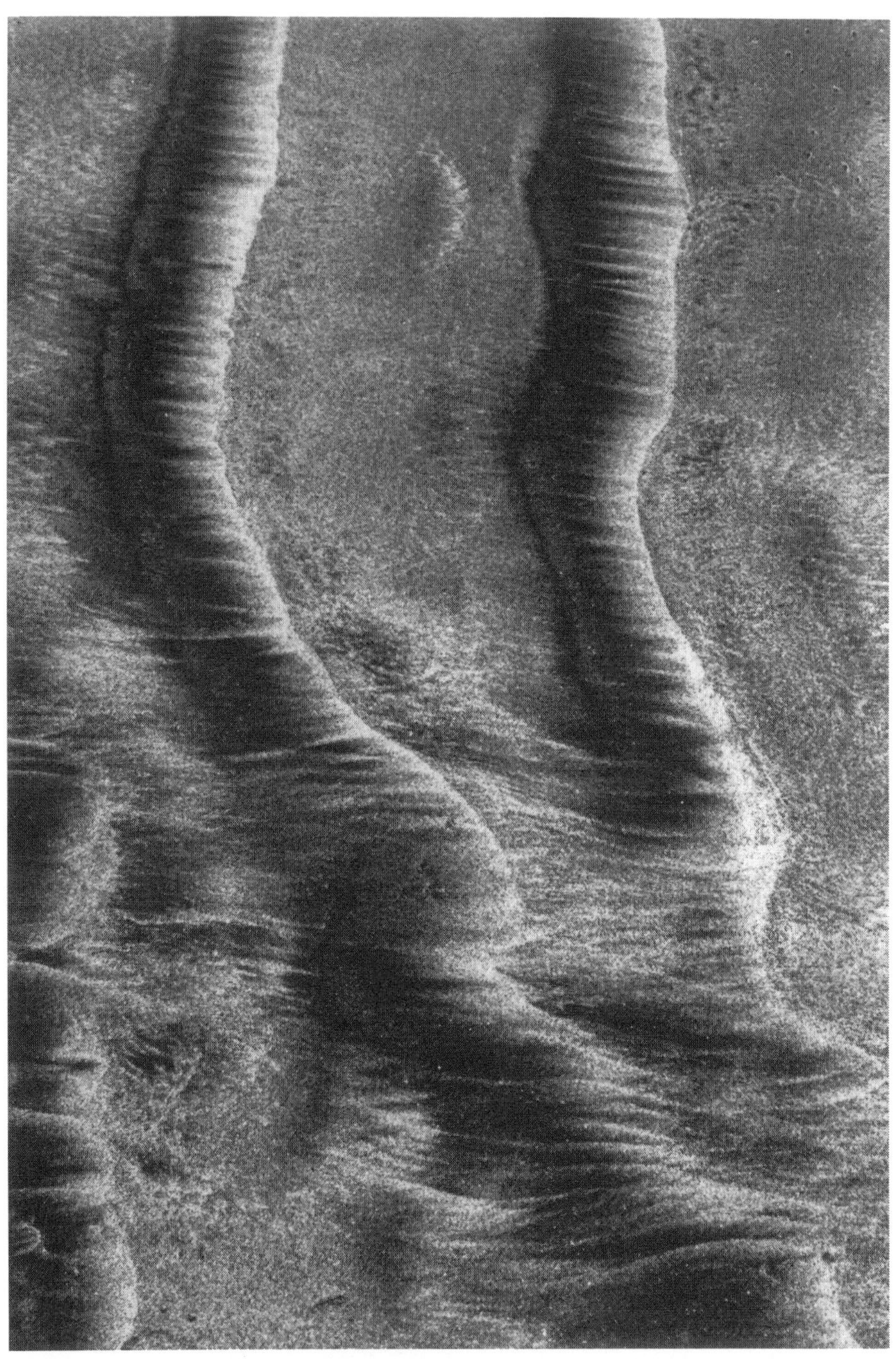

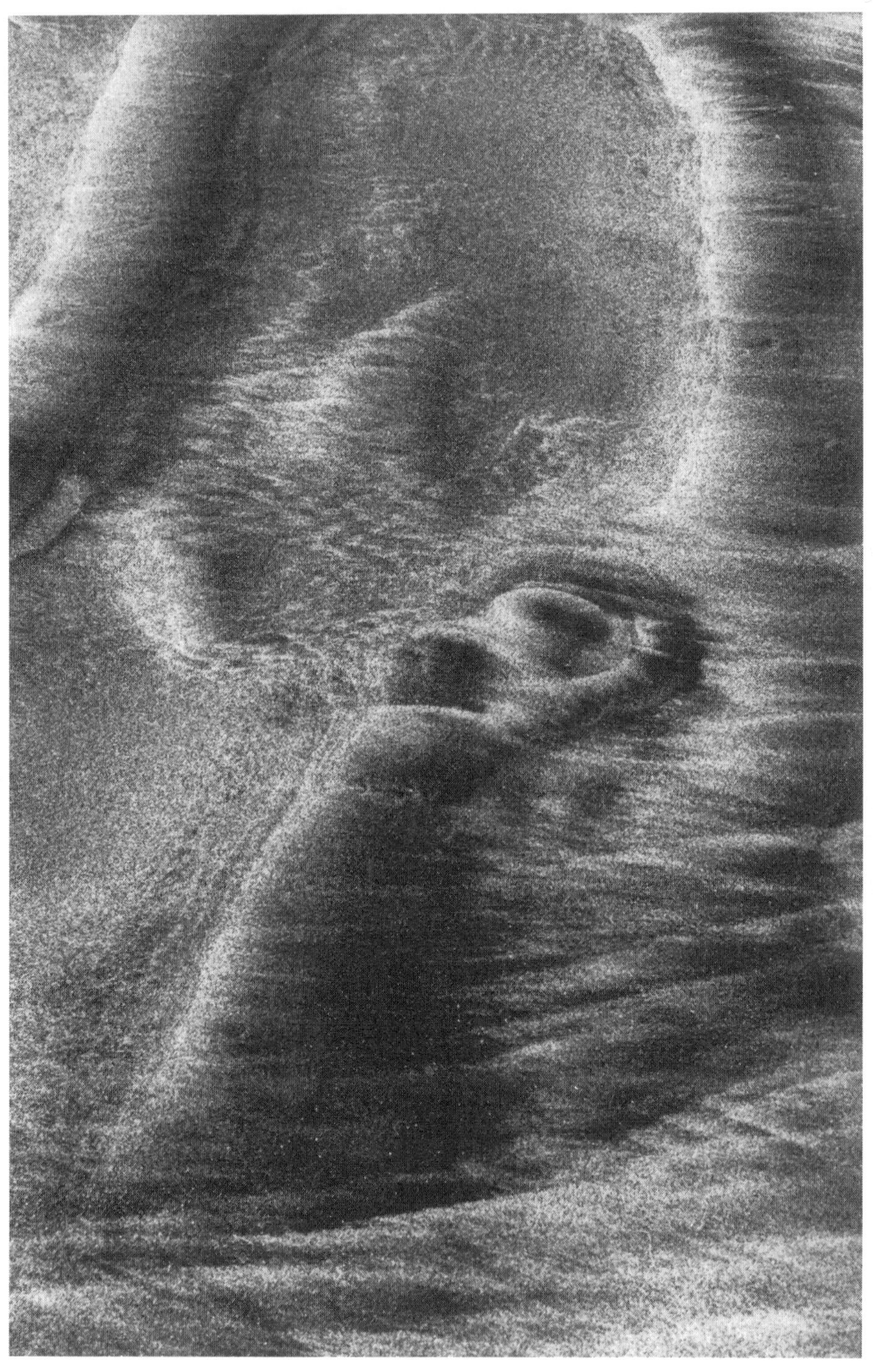

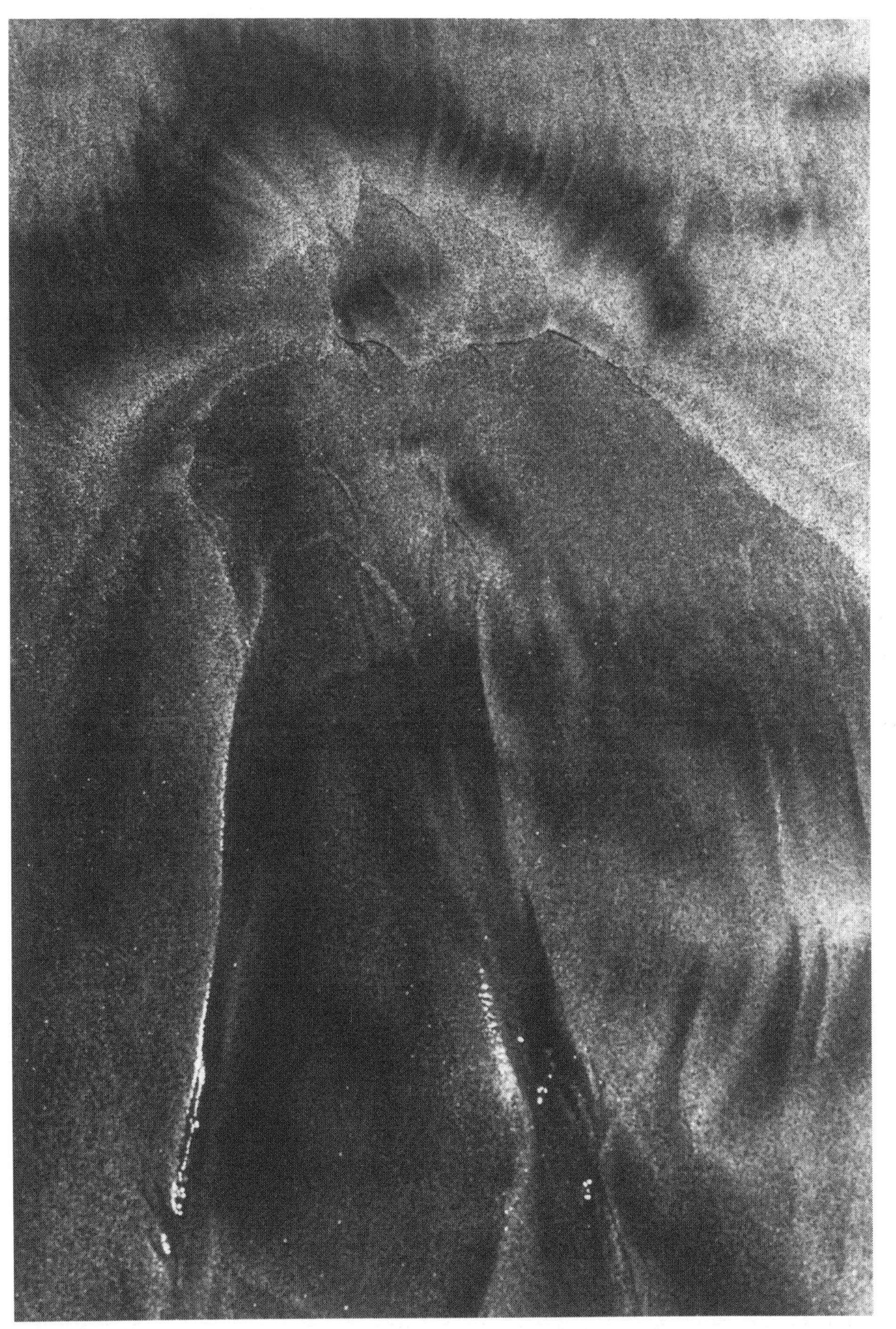

Summer, 1974

What *is* this?

Hanging out in the central square of San Miguel de Allende, I meet Diego, a friendly guy from Brazil. We hit it off and talk small talk for about twenty minutes – where we're from, what we're doing in San Miguel, good local restaurants, when he says to me, "Scott, there's one thing that I really want to know."

"What's that?" I ask.

With open hands, he reaches out with his arms and motions to everything and everyone around us as he turns in a full circle. Then he raises his arms skyward and asks, "What *is* this?"

I laugh and tell him, "That's what *I* want to know. What *is* this?"

Summer, 1974

A peyote trip in Mexico

I'm writing a novel for my Master of Fine Arts in Creative Writing program at The Instituto Allende. The novel takes place in Mexico and one of the characters is going to take peyote. I want the scene to be as authentic as possible so I ask Jack, a friend of mine, if he knows where I can get some peyote. Jack is studying painting at The Instituto Allende.

Two weeks later, Jack tells me that his friends, Francisco and Maria, are going to take peyote on Saturday in the canyon, about ten miles from San Miguel. I know both of them from the Instituto. Jack is invited to join them and asks if I can come along. They say yes. Jack gives me their address and says I should be there at ten in the morning.

Saturday morning at ten, I knock on the front door of Maria and

Francisco's house and they greet me with smiles. Jack is already there.

We spend a few minutes talking about our classes and a trip that Francisco and Maria took to Oaxaca. Maria asks where I live. I tell her "Fifty-nine Calle San Francisco. Stop by sometime."

It's a friendly group. We sit around a table on which there are four large glasses of orange juice in front of four plates. Each plate has three tops of peyote cacti on it.

Maria says, "Chew each peyote top thoroughly and when you swallow, I suggest a sip of orange juice as a chaser. Shall we begin?"

Peyote is the most wretched-tasting edible I've ever eaten.

An hour and a half later, the four of us arrive in three cars and park in a cleared, dirt area at the top of the canyon. Jack and Francisco have sketch pads and color pencils in backpacks. Maria, a photographer, has her camera. I have a thermos of water and a legal pad and pen in an over-the-shoulder Mexican bag.

We get out of the car and look across the top of the canyon, which is about a mile of stones. wildflowers, scrub and cacti. We all feel the effects of the peyote coming on. I certainly do. My senses have intensified and my consciousness is inseparable from the natural world around me. Everything living and inert resonates with the same shimmering bluish-white light and energy.

It doesn't feel like I'm taking a peyote trip. It feels like peyote, the spirit of the plant, Mescalito, is taking me on a trip. I'm beginning to experience an answer to the question the Brazilian man asked me in the plaza: "What *is* this?" The answer? There *is* no answer. Reality is too unfathomably mysterious for there to be an answer.

As the four of us walk toward a dirt path that will take us down a sloping incline into the canyon, Maria sees a tarantula walking about fifteen feet ahead of us. She hurries close to it with her camera and takes a photograph. Then, walking backwards in front of the tarantula, she takes another photograph before backing into a small cactus. She cries out and steps aside as the tarantula walks ahead of us onto the dirt path that leads over the canyon's edge into the canyon.

Maria pulls cactus needles from a pants leg and assures us that she's OK. We walk on the dirt path that takes us into the canyon. The path winds around rock outcroppings, some as tall as six feet. Francisco and

Maria lead the way, followed by Jack and me.

Half way down the path into the canyon, Francisco suddenly stops walking. He turns to us and says, “Don’t move. There’s a snake on the path. Back up.”

We walk backwards about six feet and stand so we can see the beautiful coral snake stretched across the path in front of us. The only movement by the snake is the flicking of its tongue.

Francisco says. “Let’s walk off the path and go around the snake.” We do so and continue our descent into the canyon.

Two-thirds of the way to the canyon floor, I see a tree with shade and I sit beneath it. I reach into the bag I’m carrying and take out my yellow legal pad and a pen, but I don’t feel like writing.

My novel seems irrelevant right now. I return the pad and pen to my bag. All I want is the experience of my peyote trip. I sit quietly and experience myself as an inseparable part of the consciousness that is everything I see.

I watch as Jack finds a place in shade off the path below me. He settles in and begins to draw on his sketch pad.

Francisco sits in front of a large boulder on the floor of the canyon. He draws on a sketch pad while Maria walks nearby, photographing what interests her. The afternoon passes timelessly.

Around four in the afternoon, three large black birds circle twice over our heads. I call down to them. “I think we should leave the canyon now. Let’s head up the path to our cars.” They call back, “OK.”

I stand and while taking a last look at the canyon, a brightly-colored hummingbird flies in front of me and before flying away, makes several passes at the red, yellow, and white flowers embroidered on the Guatemalan shirt I’m wearing.

Walking out of the canyon is more difficult than walking in. It feels as if I’m struggling to overcome something that’s pulling me back from the canyon below.

When I get to the top of the canyon, the force resisting my forward motion disappears and I walk easily to my car.

Jack appears a few minutes later and walks quickly to me. He asks, “When you were walking on the path out of the canyon, did you feel something pulling you from behind?”

"Yes," I say. "What was that?"

He shrugs. "I don't know."

Francisco and Maria appear about ten minutes later and hurry to where we stand. They're both out of breath. Maria asks, "Did you guys see them?"

"See who?" Jack asks.

"The brujas!" Francisco says. "We're walking up the path and we feel something pulling us back into the canyon."

"We both felt that," I say.

"Half way out of the canyon," Maria says, "we stop, turn around and look down where Francisco and I were on the canyon floor."

"We see three brujas," Francisco continues, "dressed in black, with black rays coming from them to the four of us as we climb out of the canyon."

"Let's get out of here," Jack says.

We drive the three cars back to San Miguel.

A few days later, there's a knock on our apartment door. It's Maria. She's holding two photographs in her hand. "Remember when I took photos of a tarantula heading toward the canyon?" she asks.

"Yes," I say

"Look at this first photo." She shows me a black and white print of her photograph of the tarantula.

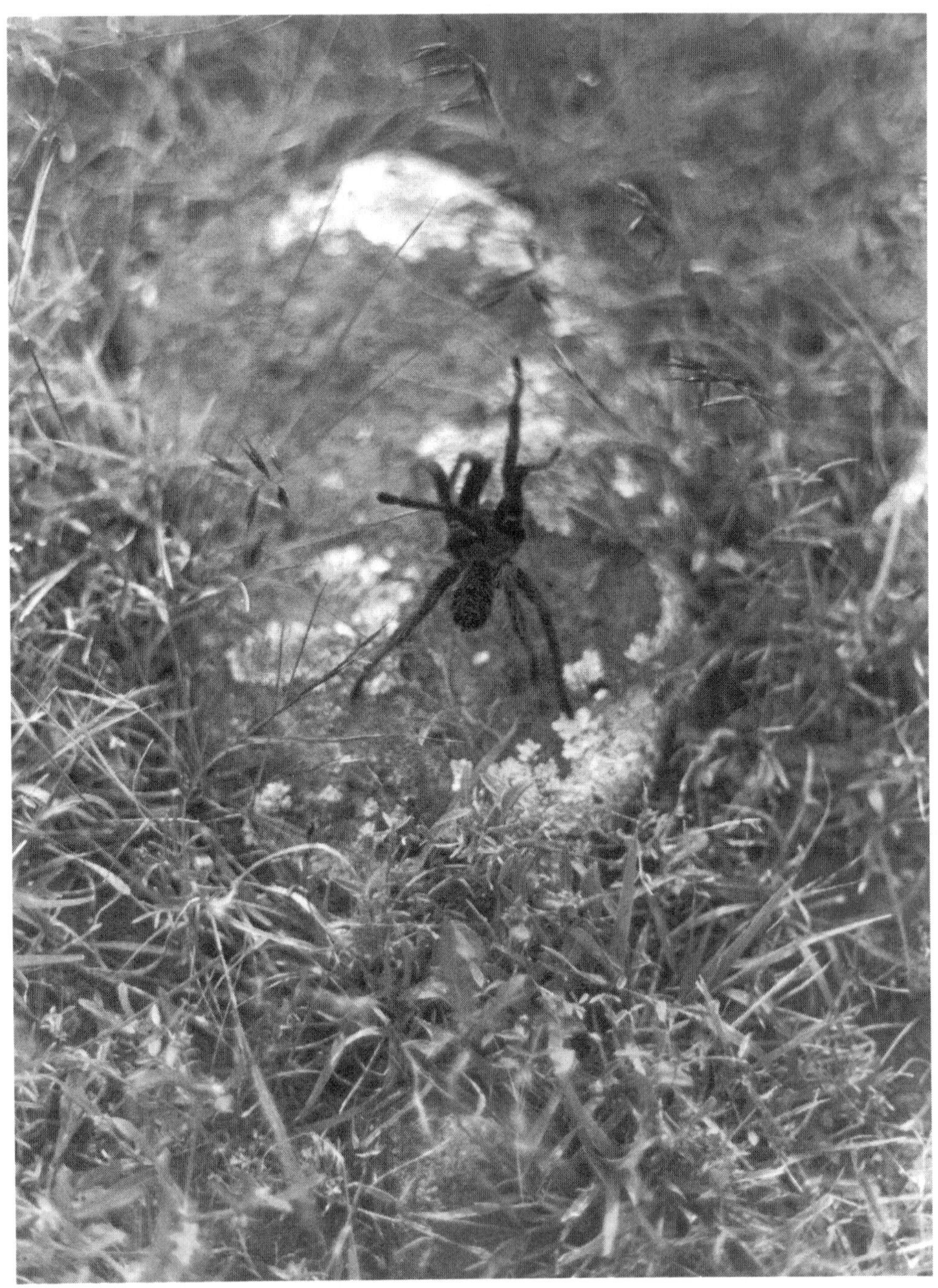

"And?" I say.

"Take a look at the second photo I took of the tarantula." She shows it to me.

"Where's the tarantula," I ask.

She says, "It's almost entirely gone. Look closely. In its place, I see a bruja's face." She points to the right side of the photo.

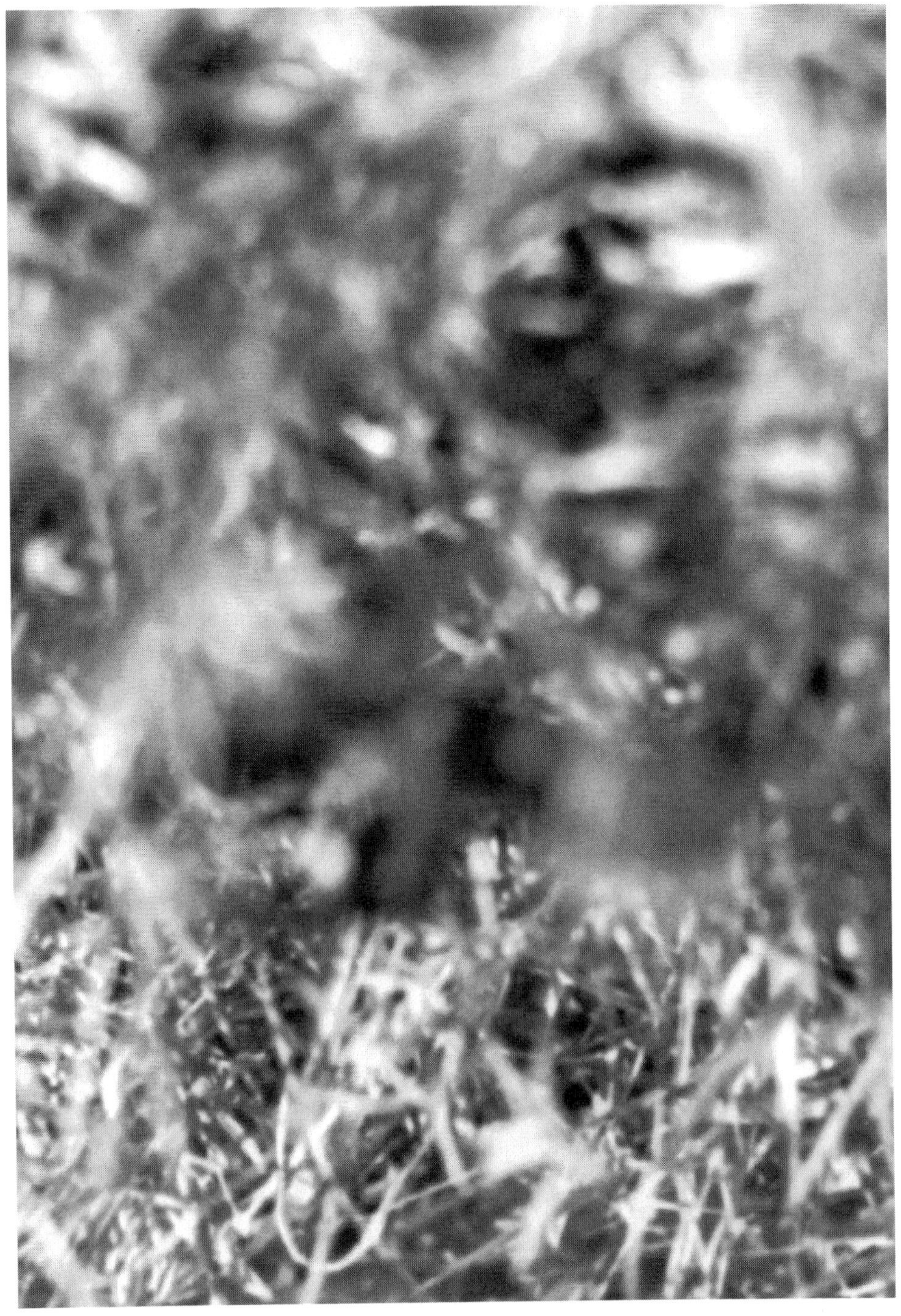

"Wow," I say. "I see it."

"So do Francisco and Jack," she says.

The photos of the tarantula and the bruja quickly become part of local lore in San Miguel de Allende. The world is as you see it.

August, 1975

I'm not in the mood

Sandy and I are living in a studio apartment close to Washington Square Park in New York City's Greenwich Village.

Mid-August, early afternoon on the hottest day of the year, I've gone food shopping. I'm walking east on Christopher Street, carrying two full bags of groceries, sweating from the heat, unable to shake a bad mood caused by getting only a few hours of sleep the night before.

Someone steps up to me from behind and presses what feels like the barrel of a gun against my back. He says, "Give me your money or I'll blow your fucking head off."

I turn my head and look at him over my shoulder, hoping to get a quick read. Is he scared? Crazy? I can't tell. He's wearing a cap and sunglasses. I say, "It's a hundred degrees out, I'm carrying two heavy bags, I'm tired and you're mugging me? I'm not in the mood."

I continue to walk toward our apartment. He again presses the same object against my back and says, "Maybe you didn't hear me. I said give me your money or I'll blow your fucking head off."

I look into his sunglasses. "Maybe you didn't hear me," I tell him. "I'm tired. I'm carrying two heavy bags on a very hot day. I'm not in the mood."

His mouth opens slightly and I walk into the middle of Christopher Street. I see two men across the street who have stopped to watch the mugging. I turn back to the man still standing where he tried to mug me. He runs west on the sidewalk and dashes north on a side street.

I cross the street to where the two men are standing and one of them says, "It looked like he was mugging you."

"Yeah," I say, "he tried to."

"What happened?"

"I told him I was tired, I was carrying two heavy bags on a very hot day and I wasn't in the mood."

"Could have gone a different way," the other man says. "You were lucky."

"Yes," I agree, "I was lucky."

I walk home and put my groceries away, thinking, that was the dumbest thing you've ever done. A few days later, I buy a second wallet and put ten single dollar bills in it with a few business cards. If I'm ever mugged again, I won't hesitate. I'll give the mugger the wallet with the ten singles in it.

1976

A revolution of consciousness

There are posters around Manhattan advertising an Intensive with Swami Muktananda, a spiritual master from India, a teacher of his lineage, Siddha Yoga. The Intensive is to be held at the DeVille Hotel in the Catskills, New York. In years past, the DeVille had been a Borscht Belt hotel for comedians. No longer.

The registration fee is $90. Sandy and I consider going but decide not to, thinking the $90 fee is too high.

A few weeks before the Intensive, we go to a dinner party at a friend's apartment in Manhattan. After dinner, with dishes washed and the table where we ate wiped clean, Linda, the host, asks her three guests, Kelly, Sandy and me, if we'd like to have a séance. We all say yes.

She places a metal Postum cap at the center of the table. Then, at a distance of about fifteen inches from the cap, she encircles the cap with the twenty-six letters of the alphabet, placed in alphabetical order, with each letter written on a small, white, square card.

Half way down one side of the circle of letters, between "M" and "N," on a small, square card, she inserts the word "YES." Half way down the opposite side, on a card the same size, she places the word "No." She dims the lights and the four of us take seats around the table.

The feeling in the room is respectful and non-judgmental. An impartial observer wouldn't characterize us as true-believers, or as skeptics.

Linda begins the séance by asking for protection. She says, "We ask that only spirits who wish to guide us to our highest good be allowed to communicate with us." She then places a forefinger lightly on the Postum cap and the three of us do the same. She says, "If there is a spirit who would like to communicate with someone in the room, please move the cap to the letter beginning with that person's first name."

Though we have four forefingers placed lightly on the cap, it moves across the table as if animated by an energy separate from the four of us. It stops in front of the letter "S."

I ask, "Does this spirit want to communicate with me?"

The cap moves to the word "YES."

I say, "Please give the initials of your name."

The cap moves to the letter "M," then to the letter "F," where it stops.

I ask "Is this Michael Fried?"

The cap moves to "YES."

I'm stunned. I ask questions and the cap answers by moving to the first letter of the answer's words. I try to guess the word that the letter represents and the cap moves to "No," or "Yes." When I guess correctly, the cap moves to the next letter of its answer and I continue to guess until I get it right. Using this method, I receive Michael's message for me.

I ask, "How are you?"

He says "Good."

"Do you have a message for me?"

"Yes. Meditate. Go see Muktananda."

I ask, "Do you know Muktananda?"

He answers, "Yes. Muktananda is my guru. Muktananda is your guru too."

Whatever animates the energy that moves the Postum cap disappears, signaling an end to my communication with Michael Fried.

Linda asks, "Is there another spirit that wants to communicate with someone here?"

The Postum cap moves to "YES," and the séance continues with

Sandy, Kelly,

Linda and me for another hour.

The next day, Sandy and I send $180 to the Siddha Yoga Dham, c/o The Deville Hotel.

Two weeks later, we're standing near the front doors of the DeVille in the Catskills. A banner above the front doors reads: "God dwells within you as you." This resonates in me as truth.

After registering for the Intensive, we receive a written introduction to Siddha Yoga in which Muktananda extends a greeting. "I welcome you all with love."

I begin by reading "What Is an Intensive?" Here is an excerpt:

"The purpose of Intensives is to enhance the process of becoming more aware of our true Self. It is an instantaneous way to start on the spiritual path, as well as an easy way to deepen spiritual growth.

Everything in the world is permeated with Shakti, divine energy, consciousness. To activate and experience that Shakti in us and thereby reach the highest realm of truth is the aim of Intensives.

In an Intensive you get both right understanding and direct experience. We come to know our true Self. The Intensive gives us the experience of ourselves as God that dwells within us as our Self, dwelling within everyone and everything as everyone and everything. Tat Tvam Assi. You are That I Am."[6]

This is the revolution I've been waiting for. I feel spiritually at home here. There is a high, sweet consciousness everywhere in the hotel.

I sleep in a men's dormitory, waking every few hours until 4:00 a.m., when I dress, take my copy of *The Nectar of Chanting* and my meditation cushion and join people walking in silence to an area outside the hotel's largest room, which has been converted to a meditation hall. We leave our shoes there and enter the hall, following Intensive assistants to places on the carpet marked with tape, where we sit and meditate.

About a hundred men fill the right side of the softly lit hall. About the same number of women fill the left side. We sit in rows, with four feet empty between each row, so when Muktananda gives shaktipat, he can pass easily from person to person.

After we sit in meditation for a while, I half-open my eyes and look at an enlarged ten-foot tall, black and white photograph, hung on the wall in front of me and to the right. It's of an elderly Indian man, wearing only a loin cloth.

I catch my breath. This man, who I will later learn was Bhagavan Nityananda, Muktananda's guru, looks exactly like the man at the rest area in the Mexico countryside who replaced my smoldering battery cables with new cables that he retrieved from the otherwise empty bed of his pickup truck.

My mind is blown. I try to meditate but my thoughts dwell on the man in the photograph and the man who replaced my battery cables in Mexico.

Someone near the front of the hall plays a harmonium and everyone opens their copy of *The Nectar of Chanting* to "Shree Guru Gita." Accompanied by the harmonium, we recite the 108 verses in Sanskrit. Below each Sanskrit verse is a translation in English. When we finish, we break until 10:00 a.m.

Sandy and I meet for breakfast in the hotel's dining room. I ask her, "Did you see the large photograph hanging on the wall in the meditation hall?"

Yes," she says. "He looks like the man who gave us new battery cables when we were stuck in Mexico." She's as astonished as I am. The Intensive intensifies.

Shortly before 10:00 a.m., we return to the meditation hall and sit on the cushions we left when we went to the dining hall.

The lights dim. We chant the mantra, Om Namah Shivaya, for about fifteen minutes, and then we meditate.

Muktananda enters the hall while we're meditating. I feel his presence before I open my eyes and see him, dressed in a saffron-colored robe and knitted cap. Holding a wand of peacock feathers in one hand, he slowly walks along a row of meditating men, stopping in front of each one, giving shaktipat with the peacock feathers or a touch between eyebrows.

When he stops in front of me, my eyes are closed. He gently brushes the crown of my head with peacock feathers and touches the space between my eyebrows with a thumb. Light fills my head and my eyes close tighter.

As Muktananda moves to the person on my left and gives shaktipat, I experience a state of consciousness that feels like the essence of my being — love and joy, timeless, placeless, an inner stillness, a divine energy. The Intensive is a life-changing experience for me.

During an Intensive talk, Muktananda refers to the two wings of shaktipat. He says that one wing is the wing of shakti itself. The other wing is the continuous effort and discipline needed for shakti to be fully and experienced in a human being.

Do I have what it takes to maintain the effort and discipline needed to continuously experience shakti in me? Only time will tell.

C.G. Jung wrote that, "The privilege of a lifetime is to become who you truly are." And then there's Popeye the Sailor Man, who said, "I yam what I yam, and that's all what I am."

Summer, 1977

A chance meeting

I'm standing in front of Balducci's market, Sixth Avenue and West 9th Street in Manhattan, enjoying a morning summer breeze, feeling relaxed, feeling good.

A radiantly beautiful woman with red hair steps from the flow of people walking on the sidewalk and approaches me. She stops with her face about two feet from mine. We smile at each other.

She looks into my eyes and embraces me lovingly in her arms. I don't say "What do you think you're doing?" I don't say anything.

She gently presses her lips against mine. I figure she's mistaking me for an old boyfriend of hers. What the hell.

She parts her lips and we kiss passionately for about two minutes. Then we hug and she says, "I'm tripping on LSD."

I ask, "How's your trip?"

"Beautiful. The city is a jewel. We're all jewels."

"Have you kissed other strangers today?"

"No, just you."

"When did you take the acid?"

"Early this morning, with my boyfriend. I wanted to go for a walk. He wanted to play his trumpet. He's a musician. He's back at our apartment, 28th and Sixth."

"Are you going back now?"

"Yes. Do you want to walk with me and meet Tom?"

"Sure."

We walk north on the sidewalk. I ask, "What is your LSD trip like?"

She stops walking, touches my face and takes my hand to her face. "Everything is beautiful," she says. "You. Me. The buildings. The sidewalk."

"Are you hallucinating?"

"For a while I saw faces in the buildings, but mostly no. I'm having a wonderful day."

At 28th Street, we walk to the building where she lives, enter the lobby and take an elevator to the 4th floor. As the elevator doors open, we hear the distant sound of a trumpet, which grows louder as we walk down the hall.

She opens her apartment door and I follow her into a studio with large windows overlooking 28th Street. Standing in front of a window, facing us, is a young man with curly brown hair, playing a trumpet, wearing only boxer shorts.

He stops playing and moves the trumpet a few inches from his mouth. Then he lowers the trumpet and gives me a what's-up look.

"Hi," I say

"Who are you?" he asks.

"I'm Scott."

"Why are you here?"

I shrug. "A chance meeting."

She says, "I kissed him in front of Balducci's. He walked me home."

He plays a riff on his trumpet.

She tells me, "He'd like you to leave now."

"OK," I say, and I walk with her to the front door.

She smiles at me and says, “Trippy.”

I laugh. “Very trippy.” She opens the door and closes it behind me. I walk home.

1978

Is this the man on the wrong plane, Mommy?

We’re living in Manhattan and I decide to see if there’s interest in my photographs of sand formations. I have ten large prints made and I show them to a book publisher in Manhattan who likes them and asks to see more, taken in different locations.

Encouraged, I bring the photographs to a geologist in the Department of Geology at Rutgers University and ask where in the United States I might find similar formations to photograph. He suggests Death Valley, California, and Cape Hatteras, North Carolina.

Early December, I decide to make a trip to both places. After discussing my plans with Sandy, I phone my good friend, Hervé Villechaize, in Los Angeles, and tell him I’ll be flying there in about ten days, renting a car and driving to Death Valley to take photographs of sand formations.

“Interesting project,” Hervé says.

“It is,” I say. “Before I head to Death Valley, I’d like to spend some time with you, if you’re free.”

Hervé likes the idea. “It will be great to see you. They’re taping an episode of *Fantasy Island* at Burbank Studios so I’ll be on the set most weekdays, but you can hang out with me there, if you want.”

“Sounds good.”

“I’d like you to stay in the house on Normandie Avenue that I rent with two guys. They have the two bedrooms downstairs, so you’d have to sleep on the living room couch.”

“Not a problem for me. I’ll call you next week to let you know when I’ll be arriving.”

"Great," he says.

Hervé is an actor, three feet eleven inches tall, co-starring with Ricardo Montalbán in the popular TV series, *Fantasy Island.*

The following Saturday, I phone Hervé and tell him, "I'm taking an evening flight to Los Angeles on Tuesday and a taxi to your house. I'll arrive sometime after two in the morning on Wednesday."

He says, "I'll leave the key to the front door under a flower pot on the porch. How long can you stay?"

"I plan to fly back to New York on Monday, but you never know."

"C'est bon," he says.

"C'est bon," I reply.

I buy an American Airlines ticket to Los Angeles and decide to wait until I'm in L.A. to buy my return flight to New York, in case I decide to extend my trip.

"There's a Monday morning flight on American Airlines from Los Angeles to J.F.K.," I tell Sandy. "It arrives at four-thirty in the afternoon. I'll be on that flight and home around seven. If I need to add a day or two to my trip, I'll call and let you know."

The day before I leave for L.A., Sandy gets an idea. "How about if I drive your car to Washington, D.C., and Monday night you could see your college friend Grigsby. We'd stay in a motel overnight and Tuesday morning drive to Cape Hatteras. United Airlines has a flight from Los Angeles to Dulles Airport in D.C. that arrives at 5:00 p.m. I could pick you up at the airport."

I like the idea and we decide to do it. I call Grigsby and tell him our plan and ask if we could stop by his house around seven on Monday evening and visit for an hour or two. He says yes. I tell him I'll call before the weekend if our plans change.

I give Grigsby's address and phone number to Sandy and tell her I'll book the ticket from Los Angeles to D.C. after I get to L.A.

Tuesday afternoon I withdraw money for my trip and pack two carry-on pieces of luggage with a sleeping bag, clothing, a thermos and toiletries. That evening, I fly to Los Angeles from J.F.K. International Airport and take a taxi to Hervé's house, arriving around 3:00 a.m. The front door key is under a flower pot on the porch.

Exhausted, I enter the living room and walk past a motorcycle to a couch, but I'm too wired to get any sleep. I'm up for the rest of the night.

Before the sun rises, one of Hervé's roommates wheels his motorcycle through the living room and out the front door. I hear him ride off into pre-dawn traffic.

About an hour later, Hervé comes down the staircase, half awake. He's wearing a pair of cutoff jeans. We hug hello, happy to see each other. He heads for the kitchen, mumbling "Coffee." I sit at a kitchen table while he brews some for both of us.

We talk about *Fantasy Island.* It's a hit series and the changes it's making in his life are dramatic. Suddenly he's being asked on talk shows, and a business manager is investing his money. He has a speech therapist, a driver and his own trailer on the set. All this and he's still living in a rundown part of L.A.

His sudden fame and wealth are accompanied by a loss of personal privacy. He tells me that everywhere he goes now, people recognize him and they won't leave him alone.

He sips his espresso and talks about a recent incident on the street. A man forced him into his car and took him home to meet "the wife and kids." He was then driven back to the street where he had been accosted. I laugh but empathize with the loss of freedom caused by his fame.

After coffee, he shows me the garden he's planted in his backyard, and upstairs, his office and his bedroom, which contains a four-foot pyramid of beer cans. "An early warning system for detecting earthquakes," he says.

He introduces me to Suzanne, a former girlfriend who recently arrived from Denmark and is staying with him.

A driver in a shiny black car takes Hervé and me to Warner Brothers Burbank studios. I'm exhausted from having been up all night.

Mid-morning, during a break on the set of the *Fantasy Island* show they're taping, Hervé tells me that on Monday, they're going to tape *Fantasy Island* for a few days on Catalina or someplace else. I decide to book my return ticket for Monday. I tell Hervé and he says he's invested money in a travel agency. He asks if I'd buy my ticket home with them.

"Sure," I say. He hands me the travel agency's business card and points to a telephone on a nearby desk. He asks, "When are you going to drive to Death Valley?"

I tell him, "I'm going to rent a car on Friday afternoon, drive to Death Valley early Saturday, spend the night there, take photographs Sunday morning and early afternoon, then drive back to L.A. and leave on Monday morning.

I ask if he'd like to drive with me to Death Valley. "We could both take photographs."

He says he'd like to but he's seeing a woman in San Francisco over the weekend.

Some people can function effectively on very little or no sleep. I'm not one of them. And if on top of extreme fatigue, I'm suddenly shocked or traumatized, well, here's what happened. Nothing like it had ever happened before, and nothing like it has happened since.

As I dial the travel agency, the show's director walks on the set and talks with someone not far from me. I tell a travel agent on the phone that I'm a friend of Hervé Villehchaize and he suggested that I call to book a ticket.

Suddenly the director turns, looks directly at me and shouts, "You! Quiet on the set!"

I'm mortified. All eyes are on me. I turn away, shield the phone's mouthpiece with a hand and continue my conversation with the travel agent, speaking in just above a whisper. But I'm so shaken by the director's sharp rebuke and from lack of sleep, that I blank on my planned return to Washington, D.C. on United Airlines and mistakenly book the flight for my Monday return on American Airlines, with a 4:30 p.m. arrival at J.F.K Airport in New York.

The travel agent tells me that since I'm buying my ticket at Hervé's suggestion, they'll deliver it to his house after 5:00 p.m. on Saturday afternoon and put it in his mailbox. I leave the *Fantasy Island* set without realizing that I've made a monumental mistake, buying a return flight to New York instead of Washington, D.C.

Hervé and I have lunch together and during the day I meet his speech therapist, wardrobe attendant, and Ricardo Montalbán, his co-star.

Early Thursday morning, I'm with Hervé and Suzanne in his trailer at Burbank Studios. There's a knock on the door.

"Come in," Hervé calls.

A driver named Chad steps into the trailer and Hervé introduces him to Suzanne and me. We shake hands and I think, this guy's drunk and it's only seven-thirty in the morning.

Chad jokes with Hervé and pulls a revolver from his jacket. We're all taken aback. He grins and waves the gun casually in the air.

"It's not loaded," he says. He playfully points the gun at Suzanne and then at me. He lowers his hand with the gun, points it away from me and squeezes the trigger. A flash of orange shoots from the gun's barrel and a bullet explodes into the shag rug on the trailer floor.

"Ho!" Chad shouts. He steps back and stares at the gun. "Sorry about that. I guess it *was* loaded."

We're too unnerved to say anything. He exits quickly after telling us he'd appreciate it if we kept the incident to ourselves.

Despite the loud gunshot early in the morning, no one comes to Hervé's trailer.

"They probably think someone's filming a western at Burbank Studios," he says. He digs his fingers into the rug and finds the spent bullet, its nose now pug.

"I want to keep this as a reminder," Hervé says. "This is how close death was to us." He pockets the bullet, then finds the casing on the rug and hands it to me. "Keep this as a reminder."

I slip the casing into my wallet and focus my thinking on driving to Death Valley on Saturday.

Friday morning I'm downstairs talking with Suzanne when the phone rings. It's Hervé, calling from upstairs. "Come up here. I want to talk with you."

I walk upstairs and he's pacing back and forth in his office. "I'm going to Death Valley with you." he says, grinning. "I just made up my mind. I was all set to go to San Francisco when I thought, why spend a weekend with Barbara? She's trouble. I haven't spent time with Scott in years. He may not be back for a long time, so I decided – I'm going with you."

I'm delighted. "Great! When do you want to leave?"

"As early as possible tomorrow morning," he says, "which means we have plenty to do. We have to rent a car, buy film – I have to find my cameras, my tripod, get money, clothing, supplies, my sleeping bag, and I have to let people know where I'm going and that I'll be back Sunday night."

By early Friday afternoon, we have everything we need for our trip. We're in high spirits.

That night, Hervé takes Suzanne and me to a party. We leave after one in the morning and as we drive toward his house on Normandie Avenue, he and I have the same idea: let's begin our trip to Death Valley now.

We pack our rented car and leave at 3:00 a.m., sharing a thermos of hot coffee. The highway heading out of L.A. is thick with fog. Hervé turns on the radio, takes a harmonica from a pocket and plays along with the songs we hear.

We drive to the Mohave Desert and stop at a roadside café. It's 5:00 a.m.

"Feels great to be heading to Death Valley," I say.

He agrees. "I needed to get out of Los Angeles. The pressure was getting to me."

We walk into the café and sit at a table. A young woman wearing a name tag, "Sherry," on her white uniform, comes over and looks at Hervé. "Aren't you the guy on that show, *Fantasy Island*?"

Herve smiles. "Yeah. I'd like a cheese omelet, rye toast and a cup of coffee."

"I'll have the same."

"It's really you!" she exclaims, writing the order. She asks Hervé "Can I have your autograph?" He says yes. She hurries to the kitchen door and pushes it open. "Hey, Vinny! You got a piece of paper? The midget from *Fantasy Island* is out here."

Vinny pokes his head out the kitchen door and calls to Hervé, "Hey! You're Tattoo on *Fantasy Island*, right?"

Hervé nods and asks, "Are you the cook?"

"Yeah," Vinny says. Sherry hands him our breakfast order and he tells her, "I don't have any paper. Use a napkin and get an autograph for me, too."

With a pen Sherry hands him, Hervé signs two napkins and draws a heart with an arrow through one of them. He hands that napkin to her and says, "This one's for you." Sherry is delighted. He adds, "The other is for Vinny."

I ask Sherry, "Do you want the autograph of the driver of Hervé?" She says, "Sign Vinny's napkin." I take that napkin and write under Hervé's signature, "Scott – driver of Hervé."

We have breakfast and continue driving toward Death Valley as the sun rises. Hervé plays his harmonica and our close friendship is alive again. Everything is miraculous from any height.

We drive for three hours before stopping to stretch our legs and buy some food in a supermarket. As we enter the store, the sight of Hervé causes an immediate stir.

Employees point at him and dash off to tell their co-workers, as I push a cart down the aisles, getting what we need for our trip: oranges, bananas, nuts, dried fruit, cheese, bread, a gallon of spring water.

A young man behind a meat counter spots Hervé and leaps over the counter, shouting, "It's you! It's you! Let me shake your hand, Tattoo!"

Soon we're surrounded by people wanting Hervé's autograph and he signs scraps of paper for each one.

"Let's get out of here," he says to me. We pay and are on the road again.

"That blew my mind," he says as I drive toward Death Valley. "I had no idea the show was so popular." We joke about his supermarket reception and he dozes while I drive.

After seven hours of driving, my fatigue overtakes me. Traveling down a mountain road, for a split second I fall asleep, the car veers, I awaken, turn the steering wheel back, and hear Hervé gasp, all at the same time. He clutches his chest, chuckles and says "That was a close call."

"Sorry," I say. He pours a capful of coffee for me and I drink it quickly.

He says, "If my agent knew I was making this trip he'd really freak out. He doesn't want me doing anything. There are rules written into my contract with ABC. I'm not even supposed to fly in a plane without their permission."

We reach Death Valley and begin our search for sand formations similar to the ones I photographed in Mexico but we don't find any. We drive another five hours searching, without success.

By early evening, we're beat. We've been driving for fifteen hours.

As the sun sets, we drive into town to find a motel, but the two motels are full. While wondering where we're going to sleep that night, we're approached by two young men. They recognize Hervé and want to shake his hand. We talk for a while. They're brothers — Philip and Drew. Both are wearing warm jackets and backpacks.

"Motels full up?" Philip asks. We nod.

Drew asks, "Where you gonna stay tonight?"

Hervé shrugs.

Philip says, "I'm thinking 'bout sleeping in that Conestoga Wagon over there – the one advertising the motel."

His brother tells us, "I'm sleeping back there where the cars are."

Hervé and I leave them and walk into the motel's bar to talk things over. It's now about seven at night. We order beers and sit at a table.

A group of young men drinking at a table nearby laugh uproariously.

"That's him!" one of them says. "I know it's him!"

Ain't him," another says. "Bet you five it ain't him."

"You're on."

One of the men stands unsteadily and walks over to us. "Hey," he says to Hervé, "s'cuse me and all but we're just havin' argument 'bout whether you're that midget whatsisname on TV."

The waitress brings our beers and Hervé tells him, "I don't like people betting on me. I'm not an animal." He adds, "Besides, when a bet is made on me, I want part of the action."

"Sure, sure," the man says, "but y'are that midget on TV, aren't ya?"

Hervé nods. The man slaps his thighs and shouts, "Hot Damn!" He laughs and calls to his friend, "Y'owe me five bucks. It's him, all right."

The man returns to his table, takes five dollars from his friend and orders two beers for us. His friends laugh raucously.

When the drinks arrive, Hervé says, "We'll leave their drinks on the table. Let's get out of here."

We finish our beers and leave the bar amid calls of "Hey, Tattoo! C'mere, Tattoo!"

As I drive away, Hervé says, "Is this what my life is going to be like from now on?" We both know the answer.

I notice that we're almost out of gas. We find the town's only gas station but it's closed for the night.

A few highway miles out of town, I pull off the road into a rest area and stop. Hervé has fallen asleep in his seat. I ask myself, "Why me, God?"

"Hey, Hervé," I say, "wake up. We have to decide where we're going to sleep tonight." I shake him gently but he doesn't stir.

I shake him harder and speak into his ear. "Hervé. This is Scott. Wake up!"

He mumbles unintelligibly. I speak louder. "We have a problem. We don't have enough gas to drive to another town and find a motel where we can stay."

He rubs his eyes, half awake. "Where are we?"

"We're at a rest area about five miles out of town."

"We can sleep here," he says. He reaches into the back seat and pulls out a blanket from his duffle bag. "Good night," he says. He wraps the blanket around his upper body and falls asleep.

I consider sleeping where I am, in my seat, but I'm afraid if I doze off, I'll pitch forward and hit my head on the steering wheel. "You've got to get some sleep," I tell myself. "You've been driving for almost sixteen hours."

Hervé topples over onto my lap, fast asleep. I prop him back up in his seat. He doesn't wake up. I take off my shoes and put them on the car's floorboard behind me.

The temperature outside is below freezing. We're six thousand feet above sea level.

I step out of the car, open the car's trunk, unzip one of my carry-ons and take out my sleeping bag and the blanket Hervé handed me before we left on our trip. I spread the blanket on the macadam near the driver's-side front door, place my sleeping bag on the blanket and slip inside, with only my nose, eyes and the top of my head outside the bag. I stare at the bowl of Death Valley stars above me and before I drift off to sleep, I wonder if frost is forming on my nose.

I awaken to the soft light of an overcast day. My nose feels like it's been shot full of novocaine, but we're in Death Valley! I slide out of my sleeping bag and take in the desolate landscape.

A half hour later, Hervé awakens and steps out of the car. "Death Valley!" I call to him. He smiles and calls back, "Death Valley!"

I ask, "Are you hungry?"

He nods. "Let's have some coffee." Rummaging through the back seat, he finds his small camping stove and the thermos, which still has coffee in it. He lights the stove on the hood of the car and heats the coffee in an aluminum pan. The brew does wonders for us both, reviving the on-the-road spirit of our trip.

"I haven't been this relaxed in months," Hervé says. "I'm a happy midget."

After coffee, he walks with a roll of toilet paper over the hilly terrain. He returns, shaking his head. "I couldn't find a safe place to go. Too many snake holes out there."

We get gasoline in town, have breakfast, and drive in search of sand formations. As we slowly descend to sea level, we're struck by the beauty of one particular spot that has natural sand compositions, though not similar to the ones I photographed in Mexico.

I stop the car and we get out the cameras, tripod, film, and filters. We separate. I photograph sand. Hervé photographs the landscape.

A few hours pass and we're back on the road, heading toward Los Angeles.

I turn on the radio, Hervé plays his harmonica, and we arrive at his house in the early evening, very tired but feeling wonderful about the time we've spent together.

Hervé's Saturday mail is on a table in the living room. He hands me an envelope with my return ticket in it and says, "Let's have some pasta and a bottle of wine."

"Sounds great," I say. "I'll help you make the pasta." I place the envelope containing my plane ticket in one of my carry-on luggage.

We have dinner and a second glass of wine. He asks me, "What time are you leaving for the airport tomorrow morning?"

"Five o'clock. I have to drop off the car rental at the airport. My plane leaves at eight."

"I'll say goodbye now," he says. We hug. I thank him for allowing me to stay at his house and for being my close friend. He thanks me for being willing to rough it and have a good time doing so in his house and Death Valley. "I'm going to miss you," he says.

"I'm going to miss you too."

He goes upstairs to his bedroom. I shower downstairs and I'm too jazzed from the long drive back to Los Angeles to get more than a few hours of sleep. I get up at 3:30 in the morning, pack my carry-on luggage and place them in the back seat of the rented car. An hour later, I return the car and take a shuttle to Los Angeles International Airport.

In the airport lobby, I look at my ticket, an American Airlines flight to John F. Kennedy International Airport, departing at 8:00 a.m. I'm so tired that nothing registers.

Before passing through security, a young man chanting "Hare Krishna" approaches me, carrying a travel tote. Standing in front of me, he stops chanting and says "Hare Krishna." I reply, "Hare Krishna," He takes a book from his tote and hands it to me. It has a color drawing of Krishna on the cover. He says, "Hare Krishna," and walks away, chanting.

Waiting to board the plane, seated in a chair by the boarding gate, I read several passages in the Krishna book and I think of Baba Muktananda. I close my eyes and imagine him giving shaktipat in the meditation hall of the South Fallsberg ashram.

I board the plane to J.F.K. and sit down in a rear, aisle seat. As the plane taxis down the runway, the pilot announces over the intercom, "Welcome to American Airlines' non-stop flight to John F. Kennedy International Airport in New York, arriving at 4:30 this afternoon, Eastern Time."

I snap to. "John F. Kennedy?" I say out loud. Then louder, "John F. Kennedy?!

I unbuckle my seatbelt, step into the aisle and shout, "I'm on the wrong plane! I have to get off!" I hurry up the aisle.

A flight attendant stops me. "Go back to your seat. We're about to take off."

I plead with her. "My wife is driving from New York to D.C. to pick me up at the airport there at five o'clock. I've got to get off this plane and take the next flight to D.C."

"I'm sorry," she says, "that's not possible now. Go back to your seat."

"Can someone call my wife and tell her what's happened?"

"No. We can't do that. Take your seat and fasten your seat belt."

Everyone I pass on the way to my seat knows I'm on the wrong plane, going to the wrong city, and my wife is driving to Washington, D.C. to pick me up at the airport there. I sit down and fasten my seat belt. I'm freaked out. The plane takes off. Before it reaches cruising altitude, I've asked myself a dozen variations of "How could you have done this? Have you lost your mind?"

An hour into the flight, a woman stops by my aisle seat with her young son, who is about eight years old. He asks her, "Is this the man who's on the wrong plane, Mommy?"

"Yes, Jimmy," she says.

"You're on the wrong plane?" he asks me.

"I am," I reply.

He's perplexed. "What happened?"

I try to keep it simple. "I made a mistake. That's all that happened. Have you ever made a mistake?"

"Yes," he answers.

His mother asks, "Are you comparing not brushing your teeth one night with getting on a plane to New York when your wife is driving to Washington, D.C. to pick you up at the airport?"

"No," I assure her. "Getting on the wrong plane is a big mistake. Forgetting to brush your teeth is a little mistake."

"A very big mistake," Jimmy says.

"Yes," I agree. "A very big mistake."

"Time to go back to our seats," his mother says. "Good luck with all this."

"Thanks," I say. She and her son return to their seats.

My sense of self-competence is badly shaken. I need to know how this happened. I recall being on the phone, booking my return ticket with Hervé's travel agent, when the *Fantasy Island* director shouted at me, "You! Quiet on the set!"

I'm sure that's when it happened. My mind went blank and I bought a return to New York instead of Washington, D.C.

Knowing how it happened doesn't make me feel any better about myself. I wonder how I'll explain my blunder to Sandy. I imagine her arriving at the D.C. airport and waiting for me to get off the plane at 4:30. After that doesn't happen, I hope that she'll call my friend, Grigsby, and drive to his house.

Hours pass. I check my watch. We're scheduled to land at J.F.K in about an hour and fifteen minutes.

I try to center myself. I imagine sitting in the South Fallsberg ashram meditation hall. The lights are dimmed. Muktananda, holding a wand of peacock feathers, is giving shaktipat to people in the row where I'm sitting. He stops in front of me, brushes my forehead with the feathers and touches the space between my eyebrows. Inwardly, I ask for help.

I meditate for about a half hour and when I open my eyes, I feel a sense of calm and peace. You'll get through this, I tell myself.

I unbuckle my seat belt, walk to the front of the plane and ask the flight attendant when we're going to land at J.F.K. She tells me we're on time and should arrive in about forty-five minutes. As I walk back to my seat, someone calls to me, "Are you the guy on the wrong plane?"

"Yes," I reply, thankful that none of the people on the plane are my neighbors.

About fifteen minutes later, the plane suddenly flies into a turbulent snow storm. The "Buckle Your Seat Belt" signs light up and a few minutes later the pilot speaks on the intercom.

"Ladies and gentlemen, we're heading into an unexpected snow storm and we've been directed to fly to Washington, D.C. where we'll land in about an hour, or when given permission." The plane turns to the right and flies south, out of the storm. I'm elated and stunned by my good fortune.

Passengers are abuzz, knowing that the guy on the wrong plane is going to land where he needs to be. The seat belt sign is turned off and a passenger walks to where I'm seated. He asks, "Isn't Washington, D.C. where you're supposed to meet your wife?"

"Yes."

"So, is this just a lucky coincidence for you or what?" he asks. I shrug.

The plane flies toward D.C. and circles over Dulles International Airport in a holding pattern for about twenty minutes before landing around 6:00 p.m.

A flight attendant announces that everyone is to stay on the plane for the moment, and she'll let us know as soon as they're told how to proceed.

She walks down the plane's aisle to me and says, "We've requested that they bring the mobile stairs to the plane so you can find your wife as soon as possible. I'll let you know when the stairs arrive."

"Thanks very much!" I say.

Ten minutes later, the flight attendant stands at the front of the plane and motions for me to come up. I remove my carry-on luggage from the overhead rack and roll them to the front of the plane. The flight attendant asks me if it's OK if she lets the passengers know why I'm getting off now in D.C., in case they don't already know. I say, "Sure, go ahead."

Over the intercom, she says, "As most of you already know, the gentleman standing next to me mistakenly booked a flight from Los Angeles to New York, instead of where he wanted to go, which is Washington, D.C. We were diverted here because of an unexpected snow storm and he wound up where he needs to be, at this airport. He's getting off the plane now so he can find his wife, who was supposed to pick him up here a little over an hour ago."

I smile and wave goodbye to the passengers. They break into applause. The flight attendant opens the front exit door and I carry my luggage down the stairs and roll it into the airport.

After looking everywhere for Sandy and unsuccessfully paging her, I phone Grigsby and tell him I'm at the D.C. airport. He says that Sandy is at his house. I speak with her, apologize and say I'll tell her and Grigsby what happened when I get to his house. I take a taxi there and tell them this story.

October, 1980

From time to time, I think about the small ball of hashish

For the past four years, I've tried to maintain the practices of Siddha

Yoga, and for the most part, I've been successful. We participate in several more Intensives with Muktananda in South Fallsberg, where there is now an ashram. In 1980, we move to the Upper West Side of Manhattan and meditate at a nearby Siddha Yoga center.

Then a close friend comes to town, someone I haven't seen in years. Henry is subletting an apartment in Manhattan and he invites me to stop by. When I arrive, he offers me a Moroccan kif pipe full of hashish that he made himself in the Rif Mountains of Morocco. How could I say no? I couldn't. We smoke and have a deep and funny conversation, during which my exquisite Shakti consciousness becomes a stoned, hashish consciousness.

Before I leave the apartment, as a gift, Henry gives me a small ball of his hashish, wrapped in cellophane. Years before, he gave me a Moroccan kif pipe, which I kept in a wood box in my closet. When I get home, I put the ball of hash in the box.

I resume my spiritual practice, meditating regularly, chanting the mantra, being mindful of my actions and thoughts, but from time to time, I think about the small ball of hashish in the box in my closet.

I routinely park my 1966 Buick on the Manhattan, Upper West Side street where we live. Residents can legally park their cars there, on 87th Street, between Amsterdam and Columbus Avenues, but every Tuesday and Friday, 8:00 a.m. to 11:00 a.m., all street-parking car owners in our neighborhood have to move their car from the side of the street that street cleaners will sweep. We can double park, parallel to and blocking an exit for a legally parked car. If we do that, we leave a note on their car windshield with a phone number where we can be reached, in case the owner of the blocked car needs to drive somewhere.

Or, instead of blocking a parked car's exit and leaving a note, a car owner can choose to drive someplace from eight until shortly before eleven in the morning, when we can park on the car-free side of the street after the street cleaners have passed.

Early October, on a bright and beautiful Friday morning, I decide to drive somewhere before the street sweepers come through.

I'm about to leave our apartment at 7:45 when I make a last-minute, impulsive decision. I take a lighter from my desk drawer and the wood box from my closet.

I drive crosstown with the box to the East Side of the city and park legally on 32nd Street, between Lexington and Park Avenues. There are a few people walking on both sides of the street. I roll my front windows half way down and fill the kif pipe with hashish.

Looking at the pipe, I ask myself, "Why are you doing this?"

I answer, "Because I like it, occasionally."

I smoke a bowl and recline in my car seat. Not long after I smoke, I hear the sound of a harmonium. I look across the street and see a middle-aged man with long dark hair, wearing shorts and a gray sweatshirt, carrying a boom box that plays Muktananda reciting "Shree Guru Gita," with the volume loud. The man walks east on the sidewalk until he's almost out of view. Then he turns around and walks west until he's almost out of view, playing "Shree Guru Gita," passing back and forth across the street from me for about ten minutes before walking east and disappearing from view.

Summer, 1982

Selling art on the streets of Manhattan

For the past two years I've been teaching composition and literature at Baruch College in Manhattan. Sandy and I are still living on the Upper West Side of Manhattan. Spring semester at Baruch has ended and I'm looking for a part-time summer job.

The classified ad in *The Village Voice* reads: "Selling art to the public." It gives a phone number. I call and the man who answers sets up an interview with me for the following day at ten in the morning, The address is on the East Side of Manhattan, 28th Street. I expect that the job will be selling art in a gallery.

I'm buzzed into the lobby of a high rise and I take an elevator to the seventh floor. When the front door to apartment 7G opens, the man standing before me looks like a fifty-year-old Santa Claus, without the red suit and hat.

We introduce ourselves. His name is Ted Altman. He greets me with a smile and we immediately feel comfortable with each other. After some small talk, I ask about the gallery where he sells art. He says, "My wife, Laura Altman, is the artist. She sells her paintings in a few galleries. Two other people and I sell prints of her cityscapes on the streets of New York City."

"You sell her art on the streets?"

"Against the bottoms of buildings, mostly. I'll show them to you."

He unzips a large black portfolio and takes out eleven prints of pen and ink drawings of Manhattan cityscapes. Each one is backed by posterboard and sealed with shrink wrap: Grand Central Station, Washington Square Park, the World Trade Towers, St. Patrick's Cathedral, Times Square, Central Park, Wall Street, the Statue of Liberty, the Empire State building, the Chrysler building and the Brooklyn Bridge. Each is strikingly beautiful, capturing the majesty and romance of New York City. The drawings are all done in black and white, using the detailed style of pointillism. They're fabulous.

As Ted shows them to me, he gives me time to look at each one. They're all signed in pencil, L. Altman. Some are numbered.

I'm impressed. "These are amazing drawings."

He asks what I do for a living. I tell him I teach at Baruch College.

A few minutes later, Laura Altman walks into the room and Ted introduces us. She's friendly and as easy to be with as he is.

I tell her, "Your work is incredible."

She smiles. "Thanks. Are you going to sell them for us?"

"I'd like to." I turn to Ted. "Do you think I'd be good at this?"

He grins. "I think you'd be great at this."

I ask, "Stupid question. Is it legal?"

"Well," he answers, "the places where it's legal with a vendor license are close to the East River and the Hudson River on the West Side. Not much business there but if you sell for us, you should get a vendor license anyway at Consumer Affairs."

"What happens if I get caught selling where it's illegal?"

"You get a summons" he says, "and have to appear downtown before a judge to plead your case."

"Where would I be selling?"

"On the west sides of Fifth Avenue, mostly, and any other avenue or street between 40th and 60th. You can sell on either side of those streets when I'm not there. Other questions?"

"How much do you sell them for?"

"Twelve dollars each, two for twenty. You would buy them from me for five dollars each. Do you want the job?"

"Yes."

"Welcome aboard," he says. We shake hands.

Laura is pleased. "I think you'll like the job." She turns, walks down the hallway and enters a room.

"Get your vendor license and call me," Ted says. "Your first day or two, I'll work across from you on Fifth Avenue, in case you need my help." He adds, "Just keep a lookout for police and undercover cops and you'll find out quickly whether you have more in common with an outlaw or a banker."

I get a vendor license and the following Saturday morning at ten o'clock, I meet Ted on the steps of the midtown Manhattan, New York Public Library. He hands me a black portfolio with three of each of the eleven prints in it. I hand him one hundred and sixty-five dollars. He tells me, "Sometime during your first day, you'll meet Bob. He's the other guy selling Laura's art on the street."

We set up the cityscapes on opposite sides of Fifth Avenue near Fifty-first Street, against the bases of buildings. Car and bus exhaust hang in the summer air as people walk past me quickly on the sidewalk.

I'm there about an hour and I've sold two prints when a man walks toward me carrying a large black portfolio, identical to the one I'm using that Ted said I could borrow. The man approaches me and asks, "Are you Scott?"

"Yes."

"I'm Bob."

We shake hands. He has thick black hair under a New York Mets hat. He says, "Just so there aren't any misunderstandings between us, you and Ted work between 40th and 60th, right?"

"Right."

"I work anywhere else in the city where it's illegal."

"Understood." We shake hands and he walks away, carrying his portfolio of Altmans.

A week later, when I go to Ted and Laura's apartment to replenish my supply of Laura's cityscapes, Bob is about to leave, having restored his own supply. His hair, which was black under a hat when I met him on the street, is sandy-colored and short.

"Is that you, Bob?" I ask

"It's me," he says. He unzips his portfolio of Altman prints and takes out a black wig. "I wear this when I sell on the streets," he says. "I'm between jobs as a Wall Street trader." He puts the wig back in his portfolio and leaves the apartment.

I like selling art on the streets. Everyone is wowed by Laura's prints and I enjoy talking to New Yorkers and tourists about her drawings. My enthusiasm is genuine.

Here are a few stories from the streets during the summer and early fall of 1982.

Dancing to Aretha

I've been selling Laura Altman's cityscapes for about a month. Mid-morning, I line up my eight best-selling prints against the base of a city bank. The heat wave has broken. I talk with two women from San Francisco who have been admiring Laura's drawings. They each choose two and as they're paying me, a man in his early twenties, wearing a purple bandana over the top of his head, looks at the art and says, "Hey, man, these are great!"

On his boombox, Aretha Franklin begins singing "Respect." The young man turns up the volume and begins to dance.

There's something about Aretha. You hear her sing and you want to dance, so I start dancing also, and the two women from San Francisco lean their prints against the building and dance with me and the man with the boombox, and three people walking by join us, and we all dance until the song ends. Then, without a word spoken, the two women from San Francisco take their prints and walk away, followed by the man with the boombox and the three people passing by who all danced to Aretha.

My four-word conversation with James Baldwin

During my fifteen years as a composition and literature teacher at Baruch College, whose students are among the most diverse in the United States, I experienced the indomitable spirit of Baruch's thousands of urban students. Their parents and grandparents, and often they were from all over the world, providing an expanded educational experience, just from being together.

I made the richness of their cultures part of every class. I asked who their heroes were and those were the authors we read, including Langston Hughes, Haruki Murakami, Gabriel Garcia Marquez, and James Baldwin, their favorite. We poured over his book, *The Fire Next Time*, and the papers they wrote were some of the most brilliant I've ever read.

Learning about their lives deepened my own, inspiring me the way the great authors we read inspired them. And when we were fortunate enough to receive the inspiring figure of James Baldwin as guest speaker at Baruch College, everyone stood up and cheered like he was a rock star.

Late August, 1982, mid-morning, shortly after I set up eight cityscapes against the base of a midtown building, three people, two men and a woman, stop to look at Laura Altman's prints. One of the men turns and smiles at me.

"James Baldwin!" I exclaim.

His smile widens and he replies, "You remember!"

He and the two people he's with continue walking down Fifth Avenue. "You remember!" reverberates for me as "You remember me," and "You remember the struggle," and "Don't forget the struggle," and "Remember me and you'll know why you're selling art on the streets of Manhattan."

What's *your* story?

I'm open for business, selling Altmans lined up against the base of a building in the upper Fifties, off 5th Avenue. It's early afternoon and I'm sitting on the building's stoop, near the art.

A woman with long blonde hair spends a few minutes looking at each of the Altman cityscapes. She sits down next to me on the stoop. Her hair is disheveled. She asks, "Is that your art?" I smell alcohol on her breath.

"No," I say, "they're prints of pen and ink drawings by Laura Altman."

"They're beautiful. What's *your* story?"

"My story?"

"Yes," she says. "You should be able to tell your story in a few sentences."

I hesitate. She smiles. "If you have to think about it then you don't know your own story."

I ask, "What's *your* story, in a few sentences?"

She doesn't hesitate. "I once slept with Bob Dylan. In the morning, while we were in bed, a woman walked into the room, watered the plants and left. No one spoke."

She stands. "Gotta go." She steps into the flow of people heading in her direction.

When I first saw him, he was showing me his badge

Since starting this job in June, I have successfully avoided the police, who irregularly walk beats where I sell. I thought I had a sixth sense for knowing when a policeman would pass by, but September 8th changed that notion.

When I first saw him, he was showing me his badge. I was talking with a potential customer, who immediately walked away. The policeman looked at my vendor license and wrote a summons.

That was my last day selling art illegally on the streets of New York City. I didn't like having a badge flashed in front of my face.

I'd started teaching my fall semester classes at Baruch College, but before returning my portfolio to Ted, I decide to see what it's like to sell art with a vendor license where it's legal in Manhattan.

The next morning, after teaching at Baruch, I carry my portfolio of Altmans west from East 23rd and Lexington Avenue until I'm as far west as I can go. I'm looking at the Hudson River. I turn right and walk north past a large, abandoned wood pier. It's legal to sell here with a vendor license.

As I approach a second pier, I see a blue van with tinted windows parked on it. Two women stand near the van. Both are wearing tight shorts and tank tops. I walk to them and ask, "OK if I sell art here?"

One of them asks, "Are you a cop?"

"No."

The other says, "Customers may think you're a cop. If that happens, you'll have to leave."

I tell her, "I'll keep my distance." I walk down the pier and there isn't a wall to set the art up against so I lay eight prints out on the pier's long, thick, wood planks.

One of the women walks over to me and looks at the art.

"These are really good. How much are they?"

"Twelve dollars each. Two for twenty."

"I like them. After I turn my first trick, I'm going to buy one."

"Great," I say. She returns to the van.

A man approaches the women. He points in my direction. They talk to him. He walks to me and asks, "Are you a cop?"

"No, I'm not. I'm selling art." He looks at the art and says, "Let's see your vendor license." I show it to him. He's not convinced. He tells me, "You could be an undercover cop with a vendor license."

He heads back to the two women and talks with them. One of the women walks to me and says, "He thinks you might be an undercover cop. You have to leave now."

"OK," I say. I place the eight prints in the portfolio and head home.

A month later, I'm standing in front of Judge Bruce Wright in the downtown Federal Courthouse. Judge Wright is often referred to in New York City newspapers as "Turn 'Em Loose Bruce." His compassion and leniency for those accused of having committed a crime is legendary in New York City.

A *New York Times* article by Kia Gregory, July 31, 2012, thirty years later, would read: "To some New Yorkers of a certain era, the idea that a street corner in Harlem would be renamed after Bruce Wright, the State Supreme Court Justice, (http://www.nytimes.com/2005/03/26/

obituaries/26wright.html)might seem somewhat incongruous.

To be sure, the ceremonial renaming at 138th Street and Adam Clayton Powell Jr. Boulevard, once Justice Wright's home and power base, is meant to honor a lifetime of accomplishments, including a quarter-century on the bench.

Nonetheless, a predominant chapter in Justice Wright's judicial career was marked by turbulence and criticism over some of his bail decisions in the 1970s; he emerged from that era with an enduring nickname: Turn 'Em Loose Bruce."[7]

Standing before Judge Wright in 1982, he asks me, "Are you Charles Scott Seldin?"

I reply, "I am," Judge Wright's face, his tone of voice, his eyes, are kind and empathetic.

He looks at me. "You are cited for selling art illegally on the sidewalk of Fifth Avenue, between Fifty-second and Fifty-third Street."

"Yes, your Honor."

"Did you do that on September 8th, 1982?"

"I did."

Judge Wright pauses, then says, "It's difficult for artists in New York City. Very few make it into the galleries."

"That's right," I say. "We all deserve to be able to make a living."

Judge Wright agrees. "What is an artist to do when the only places a vendor license is legal in the city are places where there aren't people passing by to buy, is that right?"

"Yes, your Honor."

He continues, "They always make it difficult for the artists. I'm dismissing your case. I hope you find a place to sell your art that's legal."

"Thank you, your Honor, and may I say, Judge Wright, what an honor it is to stand before you and have a few words with you. I admire everything you've done for the people of our city. You have understanding and compassion and wisdom that are inspiring and just, and I want to thank you for that."

Judge Wright smiles. "I appreciate your comment."

I leave the courtroom feeling great.

1984

Our son, Jasper, is born. Every color turns brighter.

1997 and 1998

The Adolescent Psychiatric Unit

I'm hired as director of Mountain View School in Santa Fe, New Mexico. Sandy, Jasper and I move to Santa Fe from our home in Croton-on-Hudson, New York.

Mountain View School's purpose is to serve the educational needs of the inpatients and day patients, twelve to seventeen years old, who receive treatment in St. Vincent Hospital's Adolescent Psychiatric Unit in Santa Fe. The length of time that patients are in the locked unit ranges from forty-eight hours to three months.

Patients on the Adolescent Psychiatric Unit are admitted with acute psychological problems. The precipitating events and conditions are often suicide attempts, depression, drug abuse or overdose, psychosis, family and/or gang violence.

Every patient on the unit becomes part of Mountain View School. I teach classes, hire tutors, motivate, drive a hospital van for school outings and help students keep up with their homeschool assignments while they're here.

Toward the end of my work day, in a staff book that has daily comments written by the unit's psychiatrists, counselors, and nurses, I write notes about each student's academic and social progress, or lack of progress.

Here is the list of forbidden behavior by patients on the Adolescent Psychiatric Unit.

MONITORED CLOTHING

NO:

1. HATS, HAIRNETS, OR SUNGLASSES ON UNIT
2. SHORT TOPS AND MID-DRIFTS
3. SPANDEX, EXCEPT FOR YOGA AND AEROBICS
4. STEEL-TOED BOOTS
5. SAGGING PANTS
6. GIVING AWAY PERSONAL BELONGINGS
7. BLACK LIPSTICK OR BLACK LIP LINER
8. SHARING OF MAKE-UP

MONITORED BEHAVIOR

NO:

1. PHYSICAL CONTACT BETWEEN PATIENTS
2. SEX
3. DRUGS
4. THREATS
5. VIOLENCE
6. PUTTING THINGS DOWN TOLETS OR SINKS
7. ROMANTIC RELATIONSHIPS
8. SECRETS, NOTE PASSING OR WHISPERING
9. SENDING SATANIC MESSAGES OR GESTURES
10. SHOES ON THE FURNITURE
11. SMOKING OR CHEWING TOBACCO
12. BORROWING OR LENDING CLOTHES OR MAKE-UP
13. GOING INTO OTHER'S ROOM
14. SWEARING OR CUSSING
15. TALKING TO PATIENT ON ROOM RESTRICTIONS
16. TIPPING OF CHAIRS
17. RAP
18. TURNING STEREO ON OR OFF WITHOUT STAFF

PERMISSION
19. USE OF PHONES WITHOUT STAFF PERMISSION
20. PERSONAL TAPES
21. WRITING ON WALLS, FURNITURE, BODY ETC.
22. NO PATIENTS ALLOWED IN NURSES STATION
23. WAR STORIES
24. GOING TO YOUR ROOM WITHOUT PERMISSION
25. GOING TO CLASSROOM OR KITCHEN WITHOUT STAFF
26. VANDALISM
27. FOOD OR DRINKS IN CLASSROOM
28. STEALING
29. HARASSMENT OR RACISM

Through good behavior during their time on the Adolescent Psychiatric Unit, patients can advance from level 1, which requires "Completion of written assignments; staff, doctor and parental approval; reaching a score of 75% and maintaining it for 2 days — to level 4, which requires "Completion of written assignments and maintaining a score of 85% for 2 days. Patients on level 4 are reviewed daily to assess whether they are ready to be released from the Adolescent Psychiatric Unit to the care of their parents or guardians."

The stories I hear from the adolescents I work with are uniquely their own. The three stories I share with you now involved me.

Nobody believes me

Wednesday morning of my first week as director of Mountain View School, a fifteen-year-old, Zoe, is admitted to the Adolescent Psychiatric Unit.

After lunch, I meet with her in my office. She and I talk about her high school classes and the homework her parents will pick up from her school and drop off here.

I tell her, "You don't have to answer any of my questions about why you're here. That's up to you."

She cautiously asks, "What do you want to know?"

"Why are you here?"

"Nobody believes me."

"About what?"

"About the man I see near me at different times of the day and week. No one else sees him. Everyone at my school and my parents think I'm crazy."

"Do *you* think you're crazy?"

"No."

"What is it like for you when you see this man?"

"I'm scared. I don't know his intention."

"When did you first see him?"

"About three months ago."

"Are you OK with my questions?"

"Yes."

"Does the man you see have a human body the way we do?"

"No. He's a spirit but he looks like a man."

Two days later, a Friday, I'm standing outside my office, which is near a room where group and family sessions and school classes are held.

The door to this room bursts open and Zoe dashes out, saying, "He's here!" She runs down the hall and into her room. The counselor supervising a group session in the room that Zoe left steps out and sees me. She says, "Scott, Zoe's seeing the man again. Would you go to her room and check on her?"

"OK," I say. I walk to Zoe's room and knock on the half-open door. "Hi, Zoe. It's Scott. May I come in and talk with you?"

A soft voice replies, "Yes." I walk into her room and sit on a chair. She's sitting on the floor with her back against a wall.

I tell her, "Your counselor asked me to make sure you're OK. How are you doing?"

"He's here," she says. She looks to her right. "He's over there."

I look where she's looking. I don't see anything.

"Do you see him?" she asks.

"I don't."

"Nobody believes me."

"It's not that I don't believe you," I say. "I just don't see him." After a pause, I ask, "How can I help you?"

Her tone is resigned. "You can't."

We sit without talking and I consider returning to my office when I feel the strong presence of someone else in the room. I turn and look where Zoe had been looking and wonder if I'm sensing the spirit she sees, or if I'm just being empathetic and suggestable. The presence is too strong for me to believe it's the latter.

Zoe sees me looking where she said he is. She asks again, "Do you see him?"

I regret saying what I reply as soon as I say it. "I don't see him, but I do feel the presence of someone else in the room."

She leans forward and asks, "Would you tell Dr. Wallach? He needs to know what you just told me." Dr. Wallach is the psychiatrist in charge of the Adolescent Psychiatric Unit.

"Zoe," I explain, "I started my job here four days ago, running the school. I don't know how Dr. Wallach would feel about having hired me if he knew I told you I felt the presence of the spirit you see. I'll have to think about this over the weekend."

When I return to work on Monday morning, Zoe and Dr. Wallach are waiting for me outside my office. We say hello and they follow me in. I sit behind my desk. Zoe sits on one of the two chairs in the room. Dr. Wallach closes the door and sits on the other chair.

He asks me to tell him what happened. I do so. He asks Zoe what she wants to do about her situation. She tells him, "I'd like an exorcism. My parents are Catholic."

"OK," he says. "Your parents are coming tomorrow afternoon for a meeting with you and me. You can ask them then. I'll support what you want. If they agree, I'll discharge you to their care and they can arrange an exorcism. If it works, and there aren't additional issues, there will be no need for you to be here. But I'd like you to agree in writing that if an exorcism doesn't work, you'll voluntarily return to the Adolescent Psychiatric Unit for continued assessment and treatment." She says she'll do that.

Zoe and her parents meet with Dr. Wallach the following afternoon. Her parents say they'll arrange an exorcism for her and she is discharged after signing an agreement with Dr. Wallach.

A few weeks later, I ask Dr. Wallach what happened with Zoe. He tells me that she had the exorcism and hasn't seen the man since then, and she never returns to the Adolescent Psychiatric Unit.

You have to keep your clothes on

Leroy was admitted to the Adolescent Psychiatric Unit by his parents after someone in their New Mexico neighborhood phoned them and said they'd seen Leroy sitting on a merry-go-round in a grade school playground, breathing in the fumes of an open gas can.

Leroy walks and talks slower than most of his peers, but not so slowly as to appear impaired. He's gentle and obeys every rule on the Adolescent Psychiatric Unit. After almost a month of treatment and keeping up with Mountain View classes and home school assignments, he reaches level 4 and qualifies for a trip off the unit. Another patient, Eugene, is also on level 4.

Early December, with Leroy and Eugene sitting on the back seat, and Hana, an Adolescent Psychiatric Unit counselor sitting next to me on the front seat, I drive a hospital van out of Santa Fe, up Artist Road, toward the mountain trails where we're going to hike.

Half way up the gently rising mountain, I look in the rearview mirror and see Leroy take off his outer jacket, then his sweater and his shirt. "Hey, Leroy!" I say. "You have to keep your clothes on."

Hana turns around and tells him, "Keep your clothes on, Leroy, or we'll take you back to the hospital."

Leroy takes off his shoes, his pants, and his underpants. He sits naked and silent next to Eugene.

I see a place off the road where I can turn around. I do so and stop the van, facing Artist Road. As I look to my right to see if any cars are coming, the rear door behind Hana opens and Leroy jumps out of the van. He runs toward the openness of the mountainside.

"I'm going after him," I tell Hana."

"Take his clothes," Hana says. "Give me the van keys. I'll go for help."

I give her the keys, jump out of the van and race to the rear door behind her. I open the door, gather Leroy's clothes and shoes in my arms and run after him.

Leroy lopes ahead of me, past scrub, cactus, pine and juniper trees. I've never seen him move with such ease. He stops about a hundred yards ahead of me and sits under a pine tree.

I catch up to him and sit near him under tree branches, putting his clothes and shoes on the ground between us.

"How are you doing?" I ask.

He smiles. "It feels good to be free. I have everything I need. I have shelter under the trees. I have food to eat." He breaks off a small branch from the tree we're under and eats a few pine needles. "I have water from streams. I have my stories."

"Pine needles?" I say, gently. "You can't live very long eating just pine needles."

"I can for a while."

"Leroy," I say, "I really do understand your wanting to be free after spending so long on the psych unit. I want you to be able to go home, but that's not going to happen soon unless you put on your clothes and go back to the hospital with me."

"No. I'd rather be here."

We sit in silence for a long while, maybe twenty or thirty minutes, listening to the wind blow across the mountain. Then I hear something in the distance and I look toward Artist Road. A mounted policeman is riding his horse in our direction.

I tell Leroy, "There's a policeman riding a horse toward us. If you put your clothes on right now, I'll tell him everything is OK. We'll walk together to the van and go back to the hospital. But if you stay here without any clothes on, you may wind up in jail. You never know how the police are going to handle a situation like this."

Leroy stands and puts on his clothes and shoes as I walk toward the approaching horse and rider and wave hello. "Everything's OK," I call to the policeman. "It would be helpful if you would stop where you are and let us walk past you to the van." The policeman waves and does as I ask.

Leroy and I walk toward them and Leroy pats the horse's head as he walks past.

We return to the van and I drive Leroy, Hana and Eugene to the Adolescent Psychiatric Unit. On the way, Hana tells me that as she drove into Santa Fe, she saw a mounted policeman. She explained the situation to him and he followed quickly behind her on his horse as she drove the van to where she had last seen Leroy and me running.

Back on the unit, Leroy goes to his room and falls asleep. I'm left wondering what unspeakable hurt caused him to huff gasoline fumes on a school merry-go-round.

Get in the car!

Cal is thirteen years old when he is involuntarily admitted to the Adolescent Psychiatric Unit. During the three weeks that he's been on the unit, I learn that he used to live in an apartment with his father in Albuquerque, New Mexico. After his father lost his job, Cal lived with him on the streets of Albuquerque for six months, until his aunt took custody of him after his father was arrested and jailed for assaulting a police officer who stopped and questioned them.

Cal said he didn't know where his mother was. He had left his aunt's home after a few weeks and lived on the streets of Santa Fe until the police picked him up for stealing food from a supermarket. A judge sent him to the Adolescent Psychiatric Unit for assessment.

On Saturdays, Cal's aunt comes to visit him, and they seem to get along well. Dr. Wallach says that Cal has agreed to return to his aunt's house to live and has promised to return to school once he is released from the Adolescent Psychiatric Unit. He has been behaving well.

I'm planning to take level 4 patients on an outing to a local bowling alley. Two days before the scheduled trip, there's a meeting of staff psychiatrists, counselors, charge nurses and me to discuss each of the patients, as we do every week.

I talk about the bowling trip. Cal has reached level 4 and ordinarily he would be allowed to go on a trip off the unit.

Dr. Wallach asks me if I think Cal would be a flight risk if he's allowed to go to the bowling alley. I say I don't know. I read what Cal wrote when I asked him to write about his experience living on the streets with his father in Albuquerque.

"Most people would hate living on the streets because it's all about survival. The streets at night would scare them off. It can be dangerous but my father kept me safe until a cop did his power thing and they got into a fight. Before that, I was OK with street life, though every day can seem like all the days before it."

Everyone at the meeting, myself included, has mixed feelings about Cal leaving the unit to go bowling.

After we discuss Cal and the bowling trip, Dr. Wallach tells me, "You make the call, Scott. I'll support whatever you decide."

"OK," I say.

He adds, "if you take him with you, have him sign a promise that he'll do what he's asked and that he won't run away."

I ask Cal if he would like to go bowling with us. He says yes. "This place is starting to make me crazy."

He signs a promise to do what he's asked and to not run away during our bowling trip. Two days later, after lunch, I drive a hospital van to the Silva Bowling Lanes, which is located in Santa Fe off Cerrillos Road, a heavily trafficked thoroughfare with very large parking lots in front of stores and restaurants.

Sitting across from me on the front seat is Annie, an Adolescent Psychiatric Unit nurse. Sitting on seats behind us are Cal and three other level 4 patients. They're ready to have fun together and they do, without any behavior problems. I stay near Cal while they bowl. Annie takes responsibility for the other three bowlers.

After bowling, the six of us leave the Silva Bowling Lanes and walk toward the hospital van, which is parked about twenty-five feet in front of the traffic passing on Cerrillos Road.

I'm walking near Cal when he suddenly bolts toward the road. He runs, zigzagging through traffic, which stops, horns blaring, as he races to the other side of the road.

"Stay here," I tell Annie, "I'm going after him."

Dodging cars, I run across the road into a parking lot exit where a black low rider car is about to turn right onto Cerrillos Road.

I race to the driver's window and motion with my hands for him to roll down his window. He does so. He's maybe twenty years old.

Speaking very quickly, I tell him, "I work on the Adolescent Psychiatric Unit of St. Vincent Hospital. A teenager from the psych unit just ran away. I'm chasing after him. Will you help me catch him?"

He says, "Get in the car."

I hurry around the front of his car, open the passenger door and jump in. He quickly backs up his car and turns it around.

"That's him!" I say, pointing to Cal, who is sprinting away, about fifty yards ahead of us.

The driver peels out and closes in on Cal, who hears the approaching car and stops running in front of an empty store with a For Rent sign in the window.

The car stops, facing Cal, who picks up a discarded glass bottle, smashes the top on the sidewalk and waves the broken bottle at us.

I step out of the car and shout, "Put the bottle down and get in the car!" He drops the bottle and does what I say.

Sitting on the back seat next to Cal, I guide the driver to the van across Cerrillos Road. He stops his car near the van and I tell him, "Thanks. You came through big time."

"Happy to help," he says.

Cal and I get out of the car. I open a rear van door and he steps in, taking a seat by himself. No one talks as I drive back to St. Vincent Hospital and we return to the Adolescent Psychiatric Unit.

Dr. Wallach greets us and asks, "How did everything go?"

1998 through 2009

The College of Santa Fe

After the Adolescent Psychiatric Unit closes in 1997 because it is losing money for St. Vincent Hospital, I'm hired as academic coordinator and personal development coach for a government-funded Trio program at The College of Santa Fe. The program is designed to give academic and coaching support to students from low-income families, and/or the first in their family to go to college, and/or students who have a disability or disabilities.

When I'm first hired, someone in my department describes the College to me as "a funky little place." It is primarily an arts college, with about seven hundred students, many of them aspiring musicians, writers, painters, educators, dancers, singers, and sculptors. They're usually hip, white, and reveling in their newfound freedom as college students.

1999

They touched our souls

After returning from Mexico in 1974 to live in New York City again, my interest in portrait photography takes off. I photograph engaging people in Manhattan, including some well-known singers, writers, and an especially charismatic boxer.

Years later, in 1999, at Counter Culture Cafe, a Santa Fe restaurant, I have a photography show of the pioneering leaders of the counterculture that I photographed.

The week before my show, I'm interviewed by Lynn Cline, for publication in *Pasatiempo, Santa Fe's Arts & Entertainment Weekly Magazine*.

The headline of the interview is "Celebrating the portraits of turbulent times." Here are excerpts from the interview.

"Armed only with a camera, Scott Seldin ended up in some pivotal places during the 1970s, taking portraits of provocative personalities who expressed intense creativity.

Seldin didn't plan for his photographs to document the decade following the vibrant and violent anti-establishment revolution that rocked the 60s.

In retrospect, however, his black-and-white images of American icons celebrate the liberated energy and poetic passion that could only have been born of such turbulent times."

Seldin's firsthand experience of the counterculture movement only deepens the emotion of his pictures. He protested the Vietnam War, he said, and the American corporate and governmental forces that imposed a deadening grip of controlling rules and lifeless conformity."[8]

Here are five photographs from my show at Counter Culture Cafe. I share these portraits as an homage to those I photographed and to the creative trailblazers throughout history who have touched our souls and inspired us to stay involved in helping to create the world we want to live in. They've influenced who we are and the stories we have to tell, including my own.

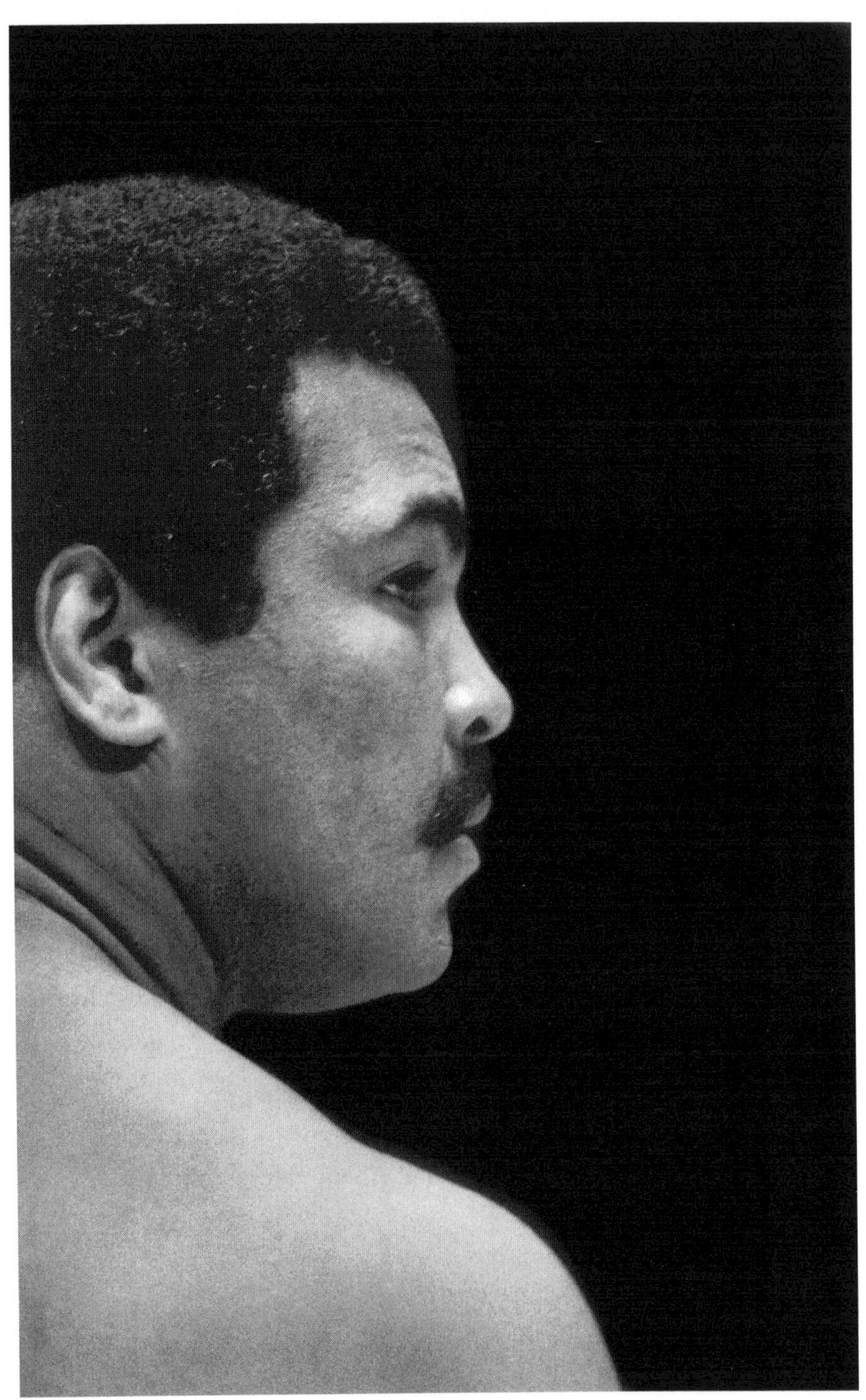

Muhammad Ali – Photographed at Madison Square Garden, Manhattan, in 1978, when Ali was training for his fight with Leon Spinks.

"Service to others is the rent you pay for your room on earth."

"Hating people because of their color is wrong. And it doesn't matter which color does the hating."

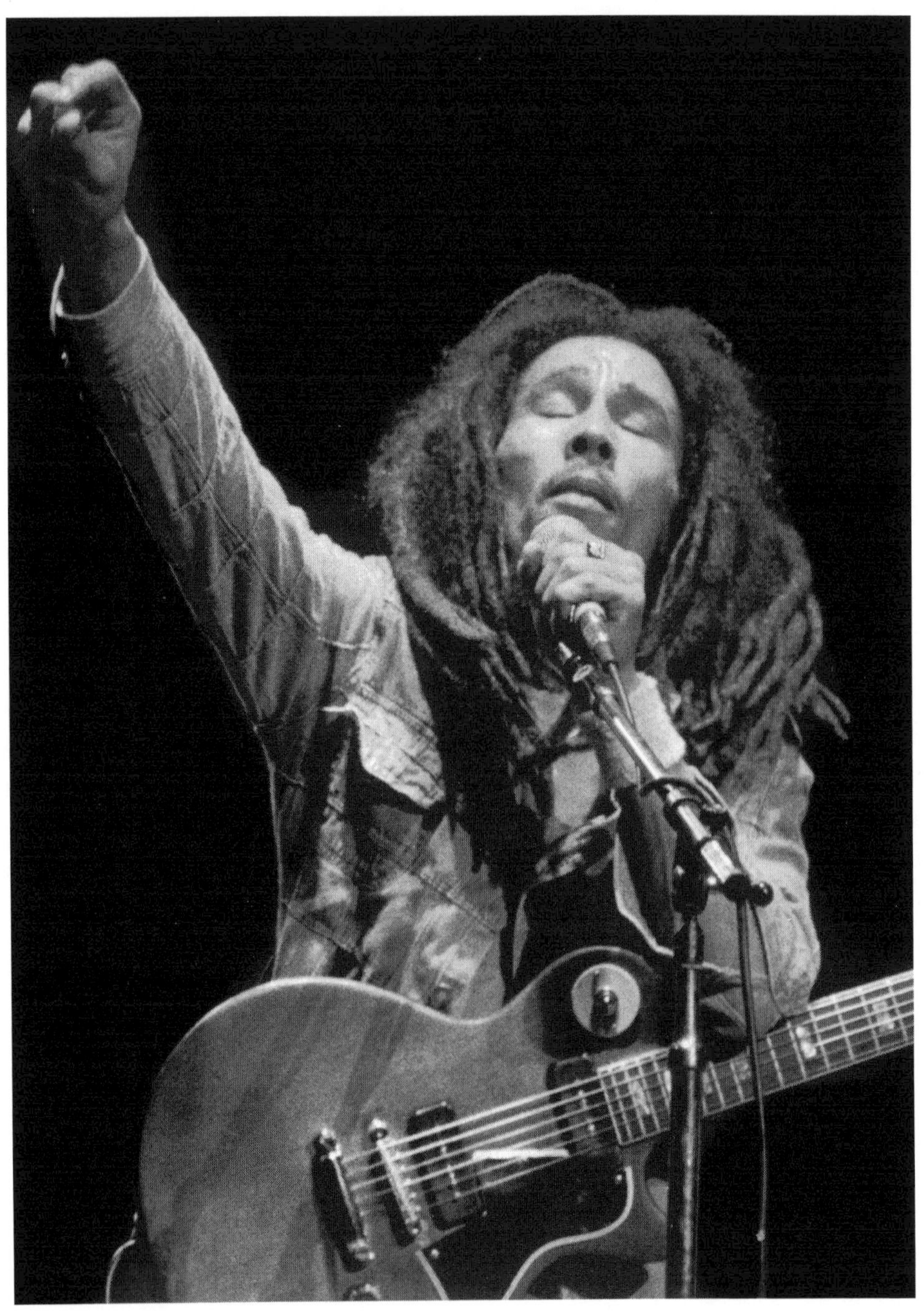

Bob Marley – Photographed in 1980 at a concert in Madison Square Garden. This photo and nine others hang in the Bob Marley Museum in Kingston, Jamaica.

"Some people feel the rain. Other people just get wet."

"Don't give up the fight. Stand up for your rights."

Patti Smith – Photographed in 1975 at a small club in Roslyn, Long Island.

"Make your interactions with people transformational, not just transactional."

"Finally, by the sea, where God is everywhere, I gradually calmed."

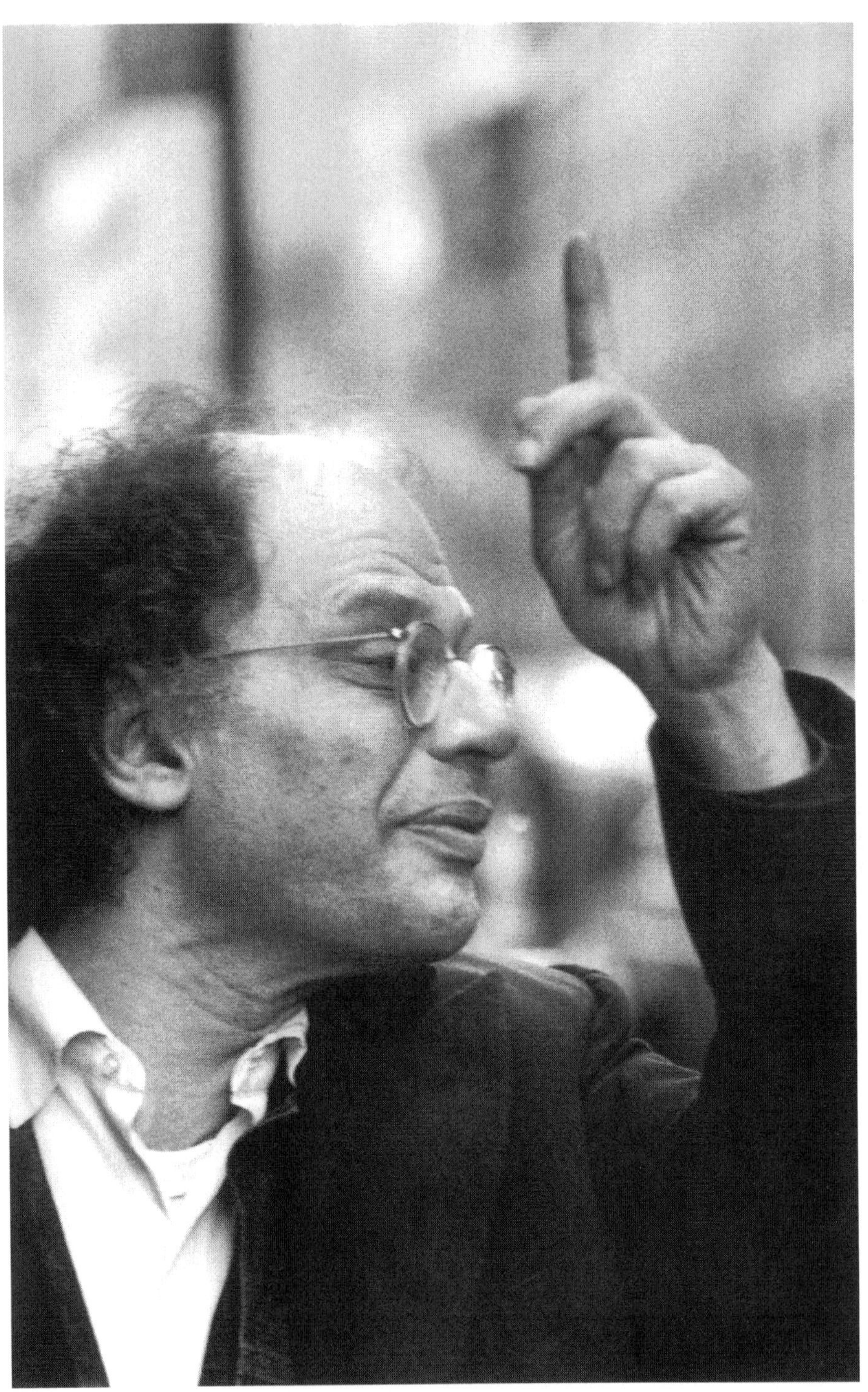

Allen Ginsberg – Photographed in 1976 outside Chumleys in the West Village of New York City, after reading his poetry at a 50th birthday celebration.

On the street, after the reading, someone asked Allen if it bothered him that I was taking his photograph. He pointed to the sky and said, "I keep my attention on God, on the universe. I don't care if he photographs me."

"Everything is holy! Everybody's holy! Everywhere is holy!"

Bruce Springsteen – Photographed while giving a surprise performance of "Heartbreak Hotel" in 1976 at New York University during a
Robert Gordon concert.

"The best music is essentially there to provide you something to face the world with."

"The great challenge of adulthood is holding on to your idealism after you lose your innocence."

Fall, 2006

Joseph is Native

In 2004, I create a college-wide mentor program at The College of Santa Fe for students who are assessed as high risk and/or are on probation. I hire and train five academically successful, personable, excellent communicators as mentors and assign four or five mentees to each mentor. For all mentees, participation in the program is required.

During the summer before each fall semester begins at the College, I send a letter to students who are going to be in the mentor program. After describing how the program works, I give them my office phone number and the name and phone number of their mentor.

Fall, 2006, Joseph's mentor, Tony, has been unable to contact him by phone – no phone number is written on his application to The College of Santa Fe. Tony writes a note to Joseph, asking that he phone him, but Joseph doesn't respond.

At the Registrar office, I get a copy of Joseph's class schedule and go to his next class as it ends. His teacher points him out to me. I introduce myself and ask if he received a letter from me about being in the mentor program. He says he did. I ask if he has a few minutes to talk in my office. He says yes. As we walk there, he's silent and I sense that he perceives me as just one more authority about to tell him what to do. He's twenty-one years old, an aspiring writer, a member of one of the eight Pueblo tribes in northern New Mexico. When I meet him, in my mind he's Native American. Shortly after we meet, he's Native.

In my office, I talk with Joseph about the mentor program and how it will benefit him.

He asks, "Is my mentor Native?"

"No," I say, "he isn't Native-American."

"Native-American?" he replies. "I'm not Native-American. I'm Native. Christopher Columbus didn't discover America. He discovered the tribes who were living here."

"Thanks for correcting me," I say.

He adds, "Our tribes are all First People. Anyone born in the United States is a Native-American."

"That's true," I say. "I wish I had a Native student to mentor you, but I don't. All students on academic probation have to be in the mentor program. You could lose your scholarship because of your grades. I don't want that to happen."

"I'm willing to be in your program but I want a Native mentor."

I reach for a solution. "I'm not Native, but given the circumstances, I could mentor you."

He looks at me as if I just don't get it. "Why do you think you would be able to connect with me well enough to mentor me? We have different priorities."

"No," I say, "I think our priorities are the same regarding your classes. We both want you to get a good education and graduate."

He explains, "I spend as much time as I can at the College, but I have to divide my time. I'm one of my pueblo's dancers and that requires lots of practice, especially leading up to festivals. And I have many family obligations. Sometimes I'm late to classes. Sometimes I have to skip class altogether because of the needs of my pueblo."

I try a bottom-line approach. "The mentor program is required for you to stay in school. We need to make this work for you. The program supports each student's individuality, their culture and traditions."

After a brief silence, he says, "I'm here to learn how to write creatively, and I want an education, but there aren't many Native students here. I don't have much in common with the other seven hundred students."

My words ring hollow as I say them. "I wish the College was more diverse."

Joseph says, "It didn't take me long to figure out that this College is mostly white professors teaching white students. If I didn't have a full scholarship, I wouldn't be here. Do you know why there aren't more Native students at The College of Santa Fe?"

"I don't know the answer to your question," I reply. "I supervise a student diversity committee and we've spoken to the president of the College and the director of admissions about enrolling more Native, Hispanic and African-American students."

"What do they say?"

"They say they support a more diverse College of Santa Fe, but they don't do anything to make it happen."

“What are you willing to do to make it happen?”

“Whatever I can.”

”No disrespect meant,” Joseph says, “but you’re an educator and my guess is you have no idea there is an Eight Northern Indian Pueblos Council about thirty miles from here.” Our eyes meet and he asks, “Would you be willing to open a discussion with the Council’s Higher Education program about increasing the number of Native students at The College of Santa Fe?”

“That’s a great idea,” I tell Joseph. “I’ll call the Council and ask if they’ll allow me to speak about this issue.”

“Good,” he says. “That means a lot to me.”

I ask, “Would you be willing to let me mentor you and have you mentor me about mentoring you?”

He smiles. “Let’s try it.” We shake hands.

The next day, Joseph stops by my office and hands me a list of his pueblo’s values. I read the list and tell him we’ll use it as a guide for our mentoring.

Joseph’s List

- The concept of sharing is a major value in family life.
- Time is secondary to people and is seen more as a natural phenomenon.
- Nature is part of living and is part of happenings such as death, birth and accidents.
- Acceptance of life is a style of being in harmony with the world.
- Family, including extended family, is of major importance and the tribe and family to which one belongs provide significant meaning.
- The basic worth of the individual is in terms of his or her family and tribe. Individual responsibility is only a part of the total responsibility concept.
- Harmony and cooperative behavior are valued and encouraged.
- Tradition is important; it adds to the quality of life in the here-and-now.

- Assertive or aggressive behavior is seen as an impingement on other's dignity.
- Respect for elders is valued, and elders play an important part in family life.

A few days later, Joseph comes to my office for our first mentor meeting. I tell him that I called the Eight Northern Indian Pueblos Council and the chairman invited me to the next meeting of the Council's Higher Education Program to speak about how we could increase the number of Native students at The College of Santa Fe.

Joseph is pleased. We talk about his classes, and when we discuss his nonfiction writing class, he says he's decided to write about our situation, with me unable to find a Native mentor for him. We're off to a good start.

Two months later, seated with twelve people around a long, rectangular table, I'm the last to speak to the members of the Eight Northern Indian Pueblos Council Higher Education Program. I tell them I'm employed by The College of Santa Fe and I asked to speak with them because a Native student at the College asked me to initiate talks aimed at enrolling more Native students at The College of Santa Fe.

After I speak, the chairman replies, "Thank you for coming and speaking on behalf of an Indian student. It has been many years since anyone from your College has shown any interest in how many Indian students attend The College of Santa Fe. Thank you for taking this first step. I ask that you tell your College president that the Council is ready to meet, should the president wish to meet with us. You have my name and phone number. Your president can contact me if there is authentic interest for starting a dialogue that will lead to more Indian students at The College of Santa Fe."

I return to Santa Fe feeling hopeful. I was received by the Council with great generosity of spirit and a sincere desire to expand the educational possibilities for their young people. Their commitment was inspiring.

Forthwith, I write a letter to our College president, reporting my meeting with educators from the Higher Education Program of the Eight Northern Indian Pueblos Council. I convey the Council chairman's invitation to begin a dialogue at their next quarterly Council meeting.

The following week, I receive a note from our College president, stating "unequivocal support for the idea of more Native-Americans at the College of Santa Fe," but adding that at this time, she has decided not to meet with members of The Higher Education Program.

It is a difficult task telling Joseph what happened, but when I do, he doesn't seem surprised, having lived with the reality of token diversity all his life. He passes his classes and is no longer on probation. I've gained as much as he has.

Spring, 2007

The Janis Joplin hot springs

As part of my job at The College of Santa Fe, twice a year I drive students in a College van on a trip designed to enrich their understanding of New Mexico's history and the three major cultures in our state: Native, Hispanic and Anglo.

After two years of visiting well known cultural sites on our trips, several students ask if they could plan our next outing themselves, and I say yes.

The trip the students plan is so popular that we begin repeating it in the fall and spring. We leave the College at nine-thirty in the morning and drive north for an hour and a quarter to Taos, New Mexico. We stop in town for an hour. Some of us spend time in Moby Dickens Books, while others explore Taos. Then we meet at the van and I drive the group west on the road heading out of town. We have lunch at Taos Pizza Out Back.

After lunch, I drive everyone to the Gorge Bridge, overlooking the Rio Grande River that flows far below us. We walk across the bridge, which was featured in the movie, *Natural Born Killers*.

From the bridge, we head to the Taos Earthships, about seven miles west. The strong appeal of the Earthships for students is that the buildings are entirely off the grid, built primarily using earth, discarded tires and cans.

The Taos Earthships website informs readers that inside the Earthship for visitors, "a self-guided tour allows you to experience a full functioning Earthship that combines passive solar architecture, thermal mass construction, renewable energy, integrated water systems that include indoor food growing, and the use of natural and repurposed materials."

A few weeks before our spring, 2007 trip to Taos, Alan, a sophomore at the College, drops by my office to sign up for the trip. We talk about where we'll be stopping and he asks if we could spend some time at the Janis Joplin hot springs before going to the Earthships.

"The Janis Joplin hot springs?" I ask. I've never heard of them.

"Yeah," he says. "Janis Joplin hung out there a lot in the Sixties and it became known as the Janis Joplin hot springs. It's on the road to the Earthships. I have directions. It's easy to find."

"Well, maybe."

He adds, "Three students going on the trip told me they'd like to stop there."

I'm open to the idea. I tell him, "If people want to stop at the springs, they should drop by my office and let me know."

During the week, three students who signed up for the trip stop by my office to say they'd like to go to the Janis Joplin hot springs. I say OK and I let everyone know we'll be stopping there and to wear a bathing suit under their clothing and bring a towel.

The morning of the trip, ten students take seats in the College van. Each carries a towel. Alan also brings his guitar and his dog, Jesse, who sits on the seat next to him. His girlfriend, Dana, sits across from him on an aisle seat.

We all introduce ourselves. Everyone's feeling good, except Gail, who sits alone in the seat behind me. I say hello to her and she seems worried. I ask if she's feeling OK. She tells me she wishes we weren't going to the hot springs. I tell her she doesn't have to go in the springs if she doesn't want to. She says she'll go in, adding that she's tired of being an outsider without friends at the College. I'd heard that she once tried to form a Young Republicans club at The College of Santa Fe and was the only student to join.

I drive the van from the College toward Taos while Alan plays his guitar and sings songs with a few students singing along.

After we spend time in Taos and have lunch at Taos Pizza Out Back, I drive everyone a few miles out of town and turn right onto Tune Road.

As I drive down the dirt road, Alan stands, holding his guitar, and tells everyone, "I don't know about all of you, but I'm going into the hot springs au natural."

Dana says, "Me too." A student sitting behind her says, "Yeah!"

Gail is rattled. Sitting behind me, she quietly repeats, over and over, "What am I going to do? What am I going to do? What am I going to do?"

I wonder the same thing. What am I going to do about this developing situation? Should I say to them, "Hey, since this is a College cultural trip, I'd like you all to keep your bathing suits on?"

I ask myself: Why risk losing your job over whether these students keep their clothes on? You coach them in your office. Will you feel comfortable working with them after this visit to the hot springs?

On the other hand, they're having so much fun – everyone except Gail, who frets on the seat behind me.

There isn't a sign saying we've arrived at the Janis Joplin hot springs but we know we're there when Tune Road ends.

I park the van on a grassy area above a sloping hillside that leads to two hot springs. The Rio Grande River flows into and over each of the adjacent springs, both of which are encircled by a low wall of stones, about twelve feet in diameter and four feet high.

Everyone but Gail and I leave the van. She now sits on the passenger seat, across from me, holding a white towel. She asks, "What should I do? I don't want to sit in a hot spring with a bunch of naked people."

I'm sympathetic. "I understand how you feel. You can stay in the van if you want, but why should you miss out on enjoying the hot springs? Maybe you should do what I'm going to do – sit with everyone in a hot spring wearing my bathing suit, not looking at anyone else."

We sit in silence for a minute, during which I consider what my defense would be if called before some College administrator with authority. I could say, "Before we took the trip to Taos, I asked everyone to wear a bathing suit under their clothes."

And he or she would say, "Yes, but when they started to take off their clothes, why didn't you stop them?"

What could I say to that? I didn't want to spoil their fun?

Yes, I decide, that's what I would say.

I tell Gail, "I'm going in the hot spring. Are you going in too?"

"Yes," she says. We leave the van and I separate from her, placing my towel, outer clothing and shoes near nine other towels, clothing, shoes, three bathing suits and the top of a bathing suit, on the stones leading to the hot spring.

Wearing my bathing suit, I enter the hot spring where nine students sit peacefully in a circle.

I say hello to everyone and sit on the stony bottom of the spring, across from Alan and Dana, who I can't help but see are naked, though I keep my gaze above them.

Gail, wearing a bathing suit, steps into the hot spring and sits next to me. I smile at her reassuringly. Agitated, she picks up a rock from the bottom of the spring, shakes it in her fist at Alan and tells him, "I feel like taking this rock and smashing it against your head." Alan doesn't react.

I tell Gail, "If you're feeling violent, you need to go for a walk or sit in the van. We'll be here for another thirty minutes."

Alan says, "Gail, I'm sorry my naked body upsets you, but it's just a body. Let's all enjoy our time together in this beautiful place."

Gail softens. "I'm sorry. I wish I'd never said that."

Alan tells her, "Not a big deal. I'm glad you're here, Gail. I've seen you around the College. What are you studying?"

"Education. I want to teach little kids."

"Beautiful," he says.

I close my eyes and meditate, happy that I don't have to look at anyone if I'm meditating. I hear relaxed talking resume and some gentle laughter. After about fifteen minutes, Gail steps out of the hot springs.

I open my eyes. She turns to me and says, "I'm going to walk around a little before we leave." She asks, "When should I be back?"

"Fifteen minutes," I say.

"OK." She says. She dries herself with her towel and heads up the hillside trail toward the van.

The ride back to Santa Fe is quiet, except for my mind, which considers the possibility that allowing students to sit naked in a hot spring on a College-sponsored trip while I sit across from them could be enough to get me fired.

As I drive, I think back to when I was hired at the College. I skimmed through the staff handbook. I don't remember reading anything that prohibited soaking in a hot spring on a College trip with some of the students naked. But did that really have to be spelled out to me?

I drive the van to the dorms at the College and when I drop the students off, I expect that by the end of the evening, everyone in the dorms will know what happened, and in the morning, Gail will meet with the dean of students to say how upsetting the trip was for her, and I'd be meeting with the dean before the end of the day.

But I was wrong.

I never heard about the trip from anyone who wasn't there. All the students who went told me how great it was. Even Gail. I feel I was protected by the students. All of them. And I think they protected Gail as well.

Spring, 2008

Where is Jesus in your life right now?

I leave the College of Santa Fe at noon and eat a sandwich as I drive to McKay's Nursery in Santa Fe to buy a wheelbarrow during my lunch hour.

My old wheelbarrow, left by the previous owner of our house, had a rusted-out hole in its bed, so I took it to the local transfer station for disposal.

I'm in a hurry. I need to get back to The College of Santa Fe for my one o'clock appointment with a student.

Inside McKay's Nursery, I take one of two red wheelbarrows,

wheel it to checkout and stand in line behind a customer who has paid for his plants and is now chatting amiably with the only cashier in the store. I sigh, clear my throat impatiently and notice that the tire of the wheelbarrow I'm about to buy is very soft. "Damn!" I say, and I consider returning it and getting the other red wheelbarrow but the customer ahead of me leaves and there are now two customers behind me and I don't want to lose my place.

I tell the cashier that while waiting in line, I noticed that the wheelbarrow's tire is very soft. She tells me it's just low on air. She asks if I have a bicycle pump at home. I say I do. She suggests that I pump air into the tire and if it leaks, bring the wheelbarrow back and get another one.

Pressed for time, I say OK. I pay for the wheelbarrow, secure it in my car's trunk, and drive to the College in time for my one o'clock appointment.

When I return home, I fill the wheelbarrow's tire with air. The following morning, the tire is very soft. I put the wheelbarrow back in my car's trunk and during my lunch hour that day, I return to McKay's Nursery.

I push the wheelbarrow into the store and tell a different cashier that I put air in the wheelbarrow's tire last night after I bought it and it leaked overnight and I'm going to get a replacement. He tells me, "You'll have to get the OK from the owner of McKay's. He's in his office. Just go down the ramp and knock on his door. Take your wheelbarrow with you to show him."

I roll the wheelbarrow down the store's ramp and stand in front of a door. I had heard that the original owner of McKay's Nursery had retired and passed the business on to his son.

From the other side of the door, I hear a man and a woman talking and laughing. I knock on the door. They continue talking and laughing. I knock again. No response. I knock a third time and an annoyed voice calls, "What is it?"

Leaving the wheelbarrow, I open the door and walk into an office. The man is middle-aged, wearing a black shirt and a crucified Jesus Christ on a silver cross that hangs from a chain around his neck. He sits behind a desk. The woman, in her twenties, sits across from him.

He says, "What do you want?"

I ask, "Are you the owner of McKay's?"

"Yes. I'm James McKay."

"Scott Seldin." I explain what happened with the wheelbarrow I bought yesterday and say I want to exchange it for another one. I add, "I was told by a cashier that I need your OK to get a replacement wheelbarrow."

He says, "Come back later. I'm busy now."

I try to conceal my annoyance. "I'm on my lunch hour. I work at The College of Santa Fe. I was told by the cashier yesterday that if the tire lost air after filling it, I could return it for another one today."

"That's right. Come back later today and I'll OK it."

"I can't come back later today. I work until five, which is when McKay's closes."

"Then come back Saturday."

I don't conceal my annoyance. "I'm asking that you open the door, look at the flat tire, OK a replacement, and I'll be on my way."

"No," he says. "It's not going to happen now."

Stay calm, I tell myself, but I ignore my advice. "I'll leave your office and come back another time, but before I leave, I'm going to tell your customers how I'm being treated by you, James McKay, and I'll ask that they go to a different nursery to shop."

I leave his office and roll the wheelbarrow up the ramp, into the store. There are about ten customers shopping.

Standing next to my wheelbarrow, in a loud voice, I say, "Ladies and gentlemen, may I have your attention? I bought this wheelbarrow yesterday, I haven't used it, and it has a flat tire. I need an OK from James McKay, the owner of McKay's Nursery, to exchange it for another one. When I asked him for his OK, a few minutes ago, he told me to come back another time, even though he's laughing and talking with someone in his office and I'm on my lunch hour from work, and all it would take is fifteen seconds to look at the tire and say, "Take another wheelbarrow." Why are we shopping here when we're treated so badly?"

I feel a sharp tap on my shoulder. I turn around and look at James McKay. "Let's take this outside," he says.

"You want to fight me over this?"

"Let's take it outside."

I follow him out of the nursery and we face each other.

"I'm a Christian," he says, "but there are times when you can't just turn the other cheek."

"And you think this is one of those times?"

"Yes."

I ask, "Are you a part-time Christian?"

"No." he answers.

"I didn't think you were," I say. "You wear a cross around your neck, so I ask you with all due respect, where is Jesus in your life right now?"

He doesn't reply.

I ask, "Do you think Jesus would want us to fight over this?"

He pauses and says, "No."

"Then let's not fight over it." I extend my right hand and we shake hands.

We walk back into the nursery and I take the other red wheelbarrow, which has a firm tire. I drive back to the College with it in the trunk of my car

Mid-summer, 2009

The most perfect thing I've ever done

Late afternoon on a hot summer afternoon, I decide to get up early the following morning and pull some weeds on our land as soon as it's light enough to see them. I roll my wheelbarrow near the weeds that I want to pull and leave it there overnight with my work gloves in the bin.

With the first light of day, I walk toward the wheelbarrow. About thirty feet from it, I notice something low to the ground on the land. When I'm about ten feet away, I see that it's a large rattlesnake, coiled, asleep on the earth.

I step back a few feet and look at the snake, knowing that I only have a few minutes before it wakes up and slithers away to its hole in the ground, which is probably on the land near our home. I don't want that.

A few years ago, I talked with a neighbor who told me that he had found a rattlesnake on his land and chopped off its head with an axe. I'm not going to do that. I've always loved almost all creatures, and though I have a fear of rattlesnakes, I would never harm them.

A plan emerges instantaneously. I roll the wheelbarrow near the garage door, which I open. Moving quickly inside, I take an empty ice chest, a shovel and a roll of duct tape, place them in the wheelbarrow's bin and close the garage door.

I roll the wheelbarrow to the left of the sleeping snake, about five feet away.

In rapid order, I remove the chest's lid and place it with the duct tape adjacent and to the right of the wheelbarrow. Three feet away and directly in front of the snake, I turn the chest on its side so its opening faces the sleeping reptile.

I consider how I'm going to scoop the snake into the chest without hurting it. I realize that this has to be the most perfect thing I've ever done.

My thinking is to shovel about one sixteenth of an inch of dirt below the snake, and, in a continuous motion, shovel the dirt and the snake into the opening of the chest.

I'm ready and focused. With the shovel drawn back for leverage, I drive it just below the snake and follow through forcefully, sending the uncoiling snake and dirt flying through the air toward the chest. The snake awakens mid-air, its rattle shaking hard as it lands inside the chest, which I quickly turn upright and cover with the lid. I hear the snake moving inside the chest, agitated, its rattle shaking warning.

I wrap duct tape around the lid and the chest, place the chest in the wheel barrow, roll it to my car and set the chest on the back seat.

As I drive toward Santa Fe, the snake settles down, with only an occasional shake of its rattle. I turn right on Artist Road and drive up the mountain, heading toward the ski lift which is about twenty miles away.

I think about the rattlesnake in the ice chest, how threatened it must feel, trapped in a dark, confined space. I realize how my fear of rattlesnakes has turned them into 'other,' judged by their means of self-protection — their rattle, their venom, their bite.

About five miles from the ski lift, I pull off the road and carry the chest to a slow-moving brook which runs down the mountain. This is an unpopulated area near a national forest.

I position the chest a few feet in front of the brook and cut the duct tape from the lid with a pocket knife. I remove the lid and gently turn the chest on its side so the opening faces the brook.

The rattlesnake moves slowly out of the chest and approaches the brook cautiously but confidently. It is a magnificent creature, with a commanding presence. Unhurried, it moves downstream across rocks that the brook flows over. I drive home and pull some weeds.

2011

The disability and ability of love

During the years that I worked at The College of Santa Fe, I coached many students who had diagnosed disabilities. This story is about someone named Daniel, but before I introduce him to you, I'll share a few relevant paragraphs from a book I wrote, *Mentoring Human Potential*, published in 2011 by iUniverse.

"Step into the world of your mentees as you step more deeply into your own world. Is your limited ability to love turning those with documented disabilities into 'other'?

Keith Murfee, (name used with permission), is a student I mentored who has cerebral palsy. I excerpt from a sermon Keith wrote and gave at his church in Washington, D.C.

'Having a disability is challenging but it shouldn't lead to a depressed life.

However, it often does because of the mindset people without disabilities have toward people with them.

A friend and mentor, Scott Seldin, suggested I write a piece entitled "The Disability of Love." I was intrigued by the concept. We all have a disability, whether we know it or not, accept it or reject it. It is the need for love. The lack of awareness we bring to our inability to love is the disability that haunts us all. It is the common ground of life."

2017

Working with Daniel

The ad on Craigslist describes him as a young adult on the autism spectrum. The job is three days a week, for a total of nine to twelve hours. After four months, it becomes four days a week, for eighteen hours.

When I arrive for an interview, two women introduce themselves and sit across from me on a couch in a Santa Fe house.

Daniel's mother, Robin, talks about the job: taking Daniel to his favorite places and activities, like bowling, thrift stores, the Chavez Recreational Center for ice skating and basketball – she also mentions movies, hiking, and lunch together in a restaurant.

Robin asks about my relevant experience and I talk about my work at The College of Santa Fe with students who had learning and social challenges.

Gina, the woman sitting next to Robin, tells me that she lives in the house with Daniel as a part-time caregiver and has a job working in a gallery.

After interviewing for a half hour, I see someone pass from a hallway entrance into the kitchen. Robin calls to him. "Daniel – would you like to meet Scott?"

Daniel walks toward us and I stand to greet him. We shake hands and he holds my right hand, gently turning it palm up. He moves the fingers of his left hand over my palm, as if reading braille. He's a tall, strong, handsome young man.

He looks at me and says, "I'm your son."

I ask, "Do you mean s-o-n or s-u-n?" He doesn't answer. Robin says, "He means s-o-n."

"It's good to meet you, Daniel," I say.

He doesn't reply. He walks back to the kitchen. Robin stands and says, "Excuse me a minute." She joins Daniel in the kitchen and quietly talks with him.

Gina asks me, "Do you have any questions?"

"Yes," I reply. "If I'm hired for the job, what do I need to know about Daniel that I don't know right now?"

She's forthright. "He sometimes has seizures and you never know when they're going to happen."

"What should I do if he has a seizure?"

"Make sure he doesn't hurt himself. Help him lie down on the floor. If someone calls the paramedics, they'll want to take him to the hospital. Don't let them do that. Help him ride out the seizure. Phone his father if you need help and he'll drive to wherever you are."

Robin calls to me, "Scott, come say goodbye to Daniel."

"OK," I say. "Good to meet you, Gina." I walk to Robin and Daniel in the kitchen.

She tells him, "Say goodbye to Scott."

I extend my right hand to shake hands but he hugs me.

"No," his mother says. "You don't know Scott well enough to hug him." Daniel and I separate and she tells me she'll let me know about the job. I leave the house and drive home.

I'm hired. When I arrive for work the following Monday, Gina has the day off from her gallery job. I drive her and Daniel in my car to the Chavez Recreational Center in Santa Fe. Robin asked her to help ease Daniel's fears about me, the new person in his life. The three of us play basketball, each shooting a ball at the same hoop and backboard.

While we take shots, Gina talks with me about Daniel in a positive way, praising him so he can hear her. I didn't know at the time how much he liked her. She is in her early thirties, about four years older than he.

I also didn't know that he didn't like me talking with her. During my first week, I would arrive at eleven in the morning and before she left for her job, Gina and I would talk for a few minutes while Daniel got ready in his bedroom to leave with me. But when he saw us talking together, his disapproval was clear, so we minimized chatting when I arrived.

During my first three weeks with Daniel, he ignores me, saying very little, keeping me shut out of his world. I'm friendly and patient but I wonder if my job with him is going to work out.

At the start of our fourth week, I'm with Daniel at the Santa Fe Chavez Recreational Center, watching him ice skate on the rink. After a half hour, he steps off the ice, walks up to me and says, "Go home. I don't want you here."

I'm gentle but direct. "Daniel," I explain, "this is my job. I'm a good person. I like you and I think if you give me a chance, you'll like me too."

His negative feelings toward me don't change until one morning while I'm driving with him on W. San Francisco Street in Santa Fe. As we approach the beautiful Cathedral Basilica, about a hundred yards ahead of us, he turns to me and says, "The cathedral looks like Notre Dame."

I'm delighted to hear his comment, which is a personal one.

"You were in Paris?" I ask.

"Fifteen years ago," he says

"With your mother and father?"

"Yes."

"You visited Notre Dame?"

"We did."

"Would you like to spend some time in the Cathedral Basilica?"

"Yes."

I park my car at a meter near the cathedral and we walk to its large, heavy front doors. I open a door and we enter. The air inside is thick with prayer.

We walk past many pews and paintings of saints on the walls and stained-glass depictions of Jesus Christ and Saint Francis of Assisi.

Daniel stops in front of the cathedral's back wall where a life-size wood statue of Jesus Christ, crucified, rises near a bank of dozens of lit votive candles.

There is a box with a slot for a dollar to buy a candle. I ask Daniel, "Would you like to light a candle and say a prayer?"

He nods yes.

I give him a dollar. He puts it in the donation box, lights a candle and places it next to the lit candles in front of him. He bows his head for a long moment before sitting next to me in a pew. We sit in silence for about fifteen minutes before leaving the cathedral.

The following morning, driving with Daniel toward town, I ask if he'd like to go back to the cathedral. He says he would, and the Cathedral Basilica becomes our second stop each day that we spend together. The first stop is Trader Joe's in Santa Fe, where we both get a sample of coffee in a very small paper cup.

After about three months of regular visits to the cathedral, Daniel and I are sitting in a pew. His head is bowed in prayer. Suddenly he stands and with arms outstretched, in a reverential voice he calls out, "Oh Jesus, we adore you!" He sits down and doesn't say another word until we're outside the cathedral.

When his mother talks with me about his love for Jesus, she's puzzled. She says he's the only one in their family like that.

Going to the cathedral softens Daniel's resistance to me.

One day, we buy tickets to see the movie "Sing" at a local movie theater. As we walk through the lobby, he asks me if I'd buy him some Junior Mints. I say sure. I buy the mints and we take seats in the first row of the theater, which has a railing running in front of the long row of seats we're in. Two feet below the railing is carpeting that extends to a very large screen.

We put our feet up on the railing and the movie begins, with only four other people in the theater.

"Here are your Junior Mints," I say, holding the box of mints near him.

"No thanks," he says. "I changed my mind."

"You changed your mind? I bought them for you a few minutes ago because you asked me to."

He shakes his head. "Too much sugar."

I ask, "How about if you just take one Junior Mint and I'll keep the rest, and if you want more you can have what you want?"

He hesitates.

"One Junior Mint won't hurt you."

"OK," he says. I give him a Junior Mint and I hold the box as the movie begins.

When the movie ends, a very upbeat Caribbean-sounding song plays through large speakers as the credits roll on the screen. The four other people in the theater leave and the song is so irresistibly joyful that Daniel stands in place and dances with abandon. I stand next to him and dance, shaking the box of Junior Mints to the music as if the box was a maraca.

Daniel vaults over the railing and dances wildly in front of the screen until the credits finish and the music stops.

I drive him home, and on the way, he asks me, "Why do I have a personality?"

I tell him, "Only an intelligent person would ask that question. I've never heard anyone ask it before. I'm going to have to think about that before I give you my opinion. And we should ask other people why they have a personality."

We do that in the week that follows, building trust and friendship between us.

2018

The ability of love

I've worked with Daniel for about a year when he asks if I would take him to the roller-skating rink in Santa Fe. I tell him I'll check with his parents. I call his mother and ask for permission. She and his father say yes. I tell Gina I'll be stopping by at 6:00 p.m. on Friday to take Daniel roller skating.

We arrive about a half hour after the rink opens for the night. Three people are roller skating around the rink as rock music plays and strobe lights flash against the walls. I immediately wish we weren't there. I've read speculation that flashing strobe lights can trigger seizures in some people on the autism spectrum.

I consider telling Daniel that this isn't a good environment for him and we should leave but he's been looking forward to this evening. I'm torn.

He rents roller skates and before he steps onto the rink, I feel compelled to say something to him about the flashing strobe lights. “Daniel, I don’t think this is the best place for you to be, with the strobe lights.”

He says, “They don’t bother me.”

“I’ve read that they may trigger seizures in some people.”

He shakes his head. “That won’t happen.”

“How do you know?”

“I want to stay.” He steps onto the rink and skates away.

I sit on one of two benches near the entrance to the rink’s fast-food restaurant and watch Daniel roller skate.

I’m thinking, maybe I should find the manager, explain the situation and ask him or her to turn off the strobe lights while we’re here. I’m told that the manager should be arriving soon.

As Daniel roller skates with strobe lights flashing, he starts waving his arms in the air and shaking his head from side to side. People who have seen us together are unfazed by this occasional behavior, but people who haven’t seen it sometimes get nervous. I’m not sure what the reaction will be at the skating rink.

There are now five people skating on the rink and four of them glance uneasily at Daniel as he skates, waving his arms in the air and shaking his head. I walk to the edge of the rink and motion for him to skate over to me. He does so. I tell him, “I think we should go now.”

“Why?” he asks.

“I think the strobe lights may be affecting you.”

“They’re not affecting me,” he says. “I don’t want to leave.” He steps back onto the rink and continues skating. I return to the bench where I’ve been sitting.

A couple in their late twenties or early thirties rent roller skates and lace them up, sitting on the bench next to the one I’m sitting on. We exchange hellos. They’re both attractive and friendly. He says to me, “We’re visiting from San Francisco. This is our first time in Santa Fe.”

“Welcome,” I say. “My name is Scott. I’m here with my friend, Daniel, who is skating.”

He says, “My name is Roland. This is Alicia.”

He's tall and wears a plaid scarf around his neck. She has long black hair that hangs to her waist.

Before they step onto the rink, Daniel skates past them, waving his arms in the air, moving his head from side to side. Roland and Alicia smile affectionately at each other and begin to skate.

About a half hour later they stop skating and talk, standing together, close to a rink wall. Then Roland skates off the rink and we exchange friendly waves as he passes near me before entering the restaurant. Alicia continues to skate, gracefully circling the rink.

Daniel's favorite movie is *Beauty and the Beast*. When we watched the movie in a Santa Fe movie theater, he knew and sang along with every song. And when I drove him home and we talked about the film, it became clear that he identified closely with both the prince, and the beast, awakened by a kiss.

Sitting on a bench near the rink's restaurant, I watch as Daniel skates over to Alicia. They stop skating and stand together as skaters pass them. He speaks close to her ear, takes her hand in his and they skate around the rink as if they are a couple.

"Oh no!" I say out loud. I stand and walk close to the rink. Daniel and Alicia skate past me, hand in hand, and he looks happier than I've ever seen him.

I turn toward the restaurant as Roland walks out, holding a tray with wrapped food and two drinks in paper cups on it. He sees Daniel and Alicia skating together, holding hands, and he says, "What?"

My mind races. Should I tell him that Daniel is on the autism spectrum and right now he's imagining himself to be a prince? I could explain that he's not delusional, he just gets into the role, but what difference would that make?

Should I walk onto the rink and tell Daniel I need to talk with him? Yes, but before I can do that, they skate closer to where we are and he tries to twirl her. They lose their balance and he crashes down hard on top of her, pinning one of her legs beneath him.

She cries out in pain and her cry doesn't stop. Daniel takes her hand and tries to console her as Roland and I dash to her side. Daniel stands as we arrive. I take him by the arm and say "Let's go over there." I walk with him about eight feet away.

Roland kneels by Alicia's side and asks, "Where are you hurt?" She says, "My left leg." He picks her up in his arms, carries her to one of the benches and gently places her on it. She lies down on the bench.

The manager of the rink appears and hurries to her side. He asks," Are you OK?"

She says, "I don't know."

"Do you need to go to the hospital emergency room?"

"No." she says, "I don't think so."

"Do you want an ice pack?"

"Yes."

He walks quickly to the restaurant and reappears a few minutes later holding an ice pack wrapped in a cloth. Roland takes it and asks Alicia, "Where should I place this?"

She puts his right hand on her left knee. "Here."

He kneels in front of her and places the ice pack against her left leg's knee

Daniel walks to them and kneels in front of Alicia, to the right of Roland. I stand near Daniel. He takes one of her hands in his two hands and says, "I'm sorry." He kisses her hand.

She smiles at him. "It was an accident. I'm going to be OK."

"Daniel," I say, "let's give them some space."

"I'm so sorry." he tells her. He stands and we walk about eight feet away.

About fifteen minutes later, Roland asks Alicia if she can stand and put any weight on her leg. She says she'll try. He helps her stand and holds her as she gingerly takes a step, then another. "It hurts," she says, "but nothing's broken and I don't think anything is torn."

We're all relieved to hear that. "Should we stay?" I ask them.

"No," she says. "I'll be OK."

I write my name and number on a piece of paper and hand it to Roland. "I'm so very sorry this happened," I say to both of them. "Call me if you decide to see a doctor." Roland thanks me, we all say goodbye, and I never hear from them.

Daniel returns his roller skates and after we get in my car, he asks me, "Are you mad at me?"

"No," I say, "I'm not mad at you. How do you feel about what happened?"

"Sad that she got hurt, but I liked skating with her."

I drive him home. Gina greets us and asks him, "How did it go?"

"Good," he says. He walks to his room and shuts the door. I tell Gina what happened, and in the morning, I email Robin and let her know as well.

When I return home, I think about Alicia and Roland and how they both handled the situation with compassion, when they could have been angry. They could have blamed Daniel for the accident and me for not stopping him when he started skating with her, but they didn't.

I think about when Daniel skated to Alicia and spoke to her, took her hand in his and skated blissfully around the rink. She allowed that to happen without awkwardness or rejection. She saw a handsome young man with a disability who wanted to hold her hand and skate around the rink as if they were a couple, and she gave him the moment he had dreamed of and, perhaps, prayed for.

May, 2018

A simple twist of fate

I'm out for my morning walk, thinking about having my car painted. It's a silver 1999 Toyota Camry with 280,000 miles, comfortable seats, a great sound system and speakers in the front and rear of the car.

Out of the blue, I think: "Wake up and smell the treason."

I stop walking and say out loud, "Wake up and smell the treason. That would be a great bumper sticker." Donald Trump is President of the United States. I walk home and find a sticker company online. Two weeks later, I open a mailed box of one hundred red, white and blue stickers that read: "WAKE UP AND SMELL THE TREASON."

I put a sticker on my car's rear bumper and whenever I see a car with a "Resist" bumper sticker, I offer one of my stickers to the driver for free. I give away dozens of stickers. Someone buys twenty-five of them at cost. Running out of stickers, I order a second hundred and distribute them.

Late summer, 2019

Covered by its green, velvet cloth

I begin to think about my viola. Though it has been in its case for decades, my bond with it is like a bond with a true love. My viola allowed me to hear who I am through the music I made when I played it.

I want to play my viola again, or sell it so it can be loved and played by someone else. Either way, it needs to be repaired.

A Santa Fe violin shop repairs my viola and I play it for several weeks but my fingers no longer have a nimble touch as they move over the strings, and I don't hear the beautiful rich sound that I heard when I played it many years ago. Reluctantly, I decide to sell my viola.

I return to the violin shop and ask the owner for an appraisal. He examines my viola, plays it briefly, and says, "Between eighteen hundred and twenty-two hundred dollars." He hands the viola to me and I place it gently in its case, covered by its green, velvet cloth.

A man leaving the violin shop, heading toward the front door, says to the owner, "See you next week." He opens the door and leaves. I say goodbye to the owner and follow the man out the door, carrying my viola in its case.

Outside, the man gets in his car as I place my viola's case on the back seat of my car and get in the driver's seat.

The man starts to drive away but stops his car behind mine. He rolls down his window. I roll down my window. He calls to me, "I like your bumper sticker." I smile and ask, "Would you like one? I had two hundred made and I give them to people who will put one on their car."

He says "Yes. I'd like one."

I reach into the back seat where I keep the stickers and take one. We both get out of our cars and I hand him the sticker.

“Thanks,” he says. “My name is Karl.”

”Scott,” I say. We shake hands.

He asks, “Do you play violin?”

“Viola,” I reply. “I had my viola repaired and I’m selling it.”

He looks interested. “I give violin and viola lessons in Santa Fe. One of my students plays viola. She’s in high school. Her parents have been renting a viola and they might be interested in buying yours.”

We exchange names and phone numbers.

The following week I leave my viola with Karl at his Santa Fe studio so his student, Jenny, can play it for a few weeks.

Two weeks later, after a phone negotiation, I meet with Karl, Jenny, and her mother, Celia, in his studio.

I’m nostalgic. I tell them that my mother bought the viola for me with money left for her when her mother died. I talk about how much I’ve loved playing it in quartets and orchestras.

Jenny is excited that her parents are buying my viola for her. I tell her, “I’m happy my viola will be with you. I have a feeling that you’ll love playing it as much as I have.”

“I know I will,” she says. “I really like your viola. I’ll take good care of it.”

Celia hands me fifteen hundred dollars. I walk to the viola, which is on a table in its open case, covered by its green velvet cloth with three yellow letters sewn into it: CSS. “You can keep the cloth, Jenny,“ I say, picking it up in my hand. “My mother sewed my initials.”

I feel very emotional. I bring my face close to my viola and stun myself by saying, “I love you.”

I walk outside with tears in my eyes. As I approach my car, Jenny runs toward me with the velvet cloth in her hands. She hands it to me. “You should have this,” she says.” I take the cloth. “Thanks,” I say. I get in my car and drive away with the velvet cloth on the front seat next to me.

January 27, 2022

I wake up and smell the treason

I'm driving home through Eldorado, New Mexico with two bags of groceries on the back seat, heading west on the main thoroughfare, Vista Grande. A white SUV follows behind me at a safe distance for several miles before suddenly closing the twenty-foot space between us to about ten feet.

At least a minute passes with the cars that close to each other. Then the driver slows behind me to a safe distance again, but not for long. This time he accelerates and follows me from about five feet behind me as we drive down Vista Grande. I feel threatened.

I make a sudden right turn onto a paved road, not far from where I live. He makes the same right turn, staying close behind me. I drive a few feet off the road and stop to allow him to pass, but he stops his car parallel to mine. He leans across his front seat and gives me the finger, mouthing hatred with his thirty-something face. I think, what if he has a gun? We live in crazy times.

With my palms up, I shrug bewilderment. He motions with both hands for me to get out of my car. Then he opens his driver-side door and starts to step out. I press my foot hard on the gas pedal and accelerate back onto the road, speeding away. He races after me in his car. I drive past the road to our house and turn left onto a dirt road. He follows me, passing through the thick dust that my speeding car kicks up. Adrenalized, I make a sharp right turn up another dirt road, and the moment he speeds past without turning, I race home and park behind some trees where my car can't be seen from the road. As I get out of my car, I realize why I've been chased. My bumper sticker: WAKE UP AND SMELL THE TREASON.

It's time. I try to remove the bumper sticker with laundry detergent. That doesn't work. I try rubbing alcohol. That doesn't work. The sticker is baked onto the car's trunk by the hot New Mexico sun.

I try an unfolded pocket knife and that works, though it takes about twenty minutes, using soapy water to remove the sticker without scratching the bumper. I'm shaken by a road-rage incident that reflects the times we're living in. Seems like I've been down this road before.

Citations

1. *Lord of the Flies*, William Goldin Published in 1954 by Farber & Farber Bloomsbury House 74-77 Great Russell Street London WC 1B 3DA, United Kingdom
2. The first eight lines of Bob Dylan's, "Masters of War," on *The Freewheelin' Bob Dylan*, released in spring, 1963, Columbia Records
3. *Autobiography of a Yogi* by Paranhamsa Yogananda A line from Chapter 1 First published by The Philosophical Library, Inc., 1946
4. Four lines from Bob Dylan's song, "On a night Like This", on *Planet Waves*, Asylum Records, released in 1974
5. Four lines from Bob Dylan's song, "Lay Lady Lay," on *Nashville Skyline*, Columbia Records, released in 1969
6. Excerpt from "What is an Intensive?" 1976 SYDA Foundation P.O Box 606 South Fallsburg, New York
7. Excerpt from an article in *The New York Times* by Kia Gregory, July 31, 2012.The New York Times Building, Manhattan, New York City, United States
8. Excerpt from an interview with Scott Seldin by Lynn Cline, "Celebrating the portraits of turbulent times," *Pasatiempo*, Santa Fe's Weekly Arts & Entertainment Magazine, September 10-16, 1999

Profile, Scott Seldin

Educator, author, photographer
Living in Santa Fe, New Mexico

After a B.A. in English from American University in Washington D.C. and an M.F.A. in Creative Writing from the Instituto Allende, University of Guanajuato, San Miguel de Allende, Mexico, Scott taught literature and composition at Baruch College for fifteen years in New York City, while freelancing as a photographer (scottseldinphotography.com). In 1982, Scott wrote *Yes, Boss*, published by Blythe-Pennington, LTD.

After moving to Santa Fe, he worked as director of Mountain View School on the Adolescent Psychiatric Unit of St. Vincent Hospital in Santa Fe, followed by eleven years as academic coordinator and personal development coach at The College of Santa Fe. At the College, he created and supervised a successful student peer mentor program and worked with students to co-produce fourteen events and projects.

The College of Santa Fe closed in 2009, and in subsequent years, Scott received training as a mediator, worked as a personal development coach, wrote *Mentoring Human Potential*, published in 2011 by iUniverse, Inc. and created Explorations of Spirit and Creativity, which offered a series of six workshops in Santa Fe with co-presenter La'ne' Sa'n Moonwalker.

In 2022, Scott published *My Out of the Blue Stories*, which he wrote during the previous year.

For information about what's new out of the blue, visit Scott's website:
outofthebluestories.com

Made in the USA
Middletown, DE
16 November 2022

15050873R00104